THE THIRD DIVE

AN INVESTIGATION INTO THE DEATH OF ROB STEWART

ROBERT OSBORNE

RMB

For information on purchasing bulk quantities of this book, or to obtain media excerpts or invite the author to speak at an event, please visit rmbooks.com and select the "Contact" tab.

RMB | Rocky Mountain Books Ltd.
rmbooks.com
@rmbooks
facebook.com/rmbooks

Cataloguing data available from Library and Archives Canada
ISBN 9781771603553 (hardcover)
ISBN 9781771603560 (electronic)

All photos have been provided by Dambuilder Productions.

Printed and bound in Canada

We would like to also take this opportunity to acknowledge the traditional territories upon which we live and work. In Calgary, Alberta, we acknowledge the Niitsítapi (Blackfoot) and the people of the Treaty 7 region in Southern Alberta, which includes the Siksika, the Piikuni, the Kainai, the Tsuut'ina and the Stoney Nakoda First Nations, including Chiniki, Bearpaw, and Wesley First Nations. The City of Calgary is also home to Métis Nation of Alberta, Region III. In Victoria, British Columbia, we acknowledge the traditional territories of the Lkwungen (Esquimalt, and Songhees), Malahat, Pacheedaht, Scia'new, T'Sou-ke and W̱SÁNEĆ (Pauquachin, Tsartlip, Tsawout, Tseycum) peoples.

We acknowledge the financial support of the Government of Canada through the Canada Book Fund and the Canada Council for the Arts, and of the province of British Columbia through the British Columbia Arts Council and the Book Publishing Tax Credit.

Disclaimer
The views expressed in this book are those of the author and do not necessarily reflect those of the publishing company, its staff or its affiliates.

This book would never have come together without the constant support of my wife and daughter—Jari and Alexa. They allowed me to obsess over the massive amount of research that had to be done and, when that was complete, allowed me to disappear for weeks on end to write the various drafts. I'll always appreciate them for being my sounding boards – and not being afraid to be bluntly honest about the work and the ideas.

Finally, I'd like to dedicate this book to my late mother and father – Margaret and Ron Osborne – who encouraged me to follow my curiosity regardless of where it took me. That was a gift that turned me into a journalist and ultimately led to this book.

TABLE OF CONTENTS

ACKNOWLEDGEMENTS

I can't thank everyone who gave me their time, their expertise and their interest in this book, but I would be remiss if I did not mention the contributions of a few people and organizations without whom this book might not have been possible: Neal Pollock, Steve Lewis and Chris Harvey-Clark for their expertise in helping me to understand the science behind the diving; the U.S. Coast Guard, Monroe County Sheriff's Office, Monroe Country Medical Examiner and Key Largo Volunteer Fire Department for their willingness to provide interviews, documents and video footage that were critical to supporting my research; Captain Hooks at Big Pine Key, for providing diving support during my two trips to the Florida Keys; and finally, the Canadian Broadcasting Corporation, Charlotte Engel and Sandra Kleinfeld; without their support for the documentary, this book would never have happened.

PROLOGUE
JANUARY 31, 2017

By all accounts, it was a beautiful day to be out on the water. The sun was shining, it wasn't too hot, there was virtually no wind and the water was calm. It was a perfect day to scuba dive in the Florida Keys. On board the 30-foot Island Hopper the *Pisces*, two divers were gearing up to go into the water. One of them was Rob Stewart, famed environmentalist and filmmaker, the other his partner, well-known rebreather expert Peter Sotis. Also on board the boat were Stewart's close friend Brock Cahill and Sotis' wife Claudia. Two crew members helped the divers – the skipper, Dave Wilkerson, and his mate Bobby Steele. This was the second day they'd been moored above a very deep wreck called the *Queen of Nassau*. They were there to gather footage for a new documentary that Stewart was filming, a sequel to his critically acclaimed film *Sharkwater*. But the diving and filming hadn't been going well.

On the previous day the four divers had completed two very deep dives – more than 200 feet down – looking for signs of a rare shark called the sawtooth. They'd found nothing. In fact, on the first dive they hadn't even found the wreck. The visibility was that limited. Today the group of divers had just completed two more extremely deep dives. The results had been the same. Something had stirred up the water and the divers could barely see more than a few feet. There might have been sharks in the mud around the *Queen of Nassau*, but sawtooths like to bury themselves on the bottom. With the best visibility, often divers only see a vague outline of their bodies or perhaps just a pair of eyes sticking up. With the current visibility, it was impossible to see them. It was also rapidly becoming apparent that filming was also a waste of time. The best shots that could have been obtained would have been murky and brief at best – perhaps a swirl of mud as the shark fled away from the divers.

After two days of diving, Stewart hadn't managed to get a single picture of a shark.

So at the end of the second day of diving, the group decided to pack it up and leave. The original plan had been to film for a third day, but given the conditions, they knew that would be a waste of time. Before they left, an anchor had to be retrieved. At the insistence of Stewart and Sotis, the boat crew had dropped a hook and line onto the wreck so the divers, carrying heavy camera equipment, could swim directly to it in the low visibility. Not an unreasonable request, given they'd missed the wreck entirely on the first day. But the crew didn't have the gear needed to go down and retrieve the hook. Peter Sotis volunteered to do the job. Rob Stewart volunteered to go with him.

Now a third dive to below 200 feet in one day is not something that many divers would consider. But this was going to be a quick down and up again, sometimes called a bounce dive: straight down, unhook the anchor and straight back up – as quickly as could be safely managed. There were some problems with the plan. The divers hadn't been on the surface very long – around 25 minutes. Normally between deep dives, safe practices suggested divers should leave at least an hour or more. Additionally, the men had done multiple deep dives over the past few days. That meant they were probably carrying a residual amount of nitrogen in their blood, even more reason to leave a good interval between dives. But Sotis and Stewart thought they'd be okay if they got down and back quickly enough.

The two men geared up and went over the side. Now one of the odd things about diving with a rebreather is that it's hard to track where the divers are when they're underwater. When divers use regular scuba gear, every time they breathe out, a burst of bubbles heads for the surface, so people on a dive boat know exactly where they are at all times – it's called surface boil. In this case, the boat couldn't track the two divers. So Wilkerson just let the boat drift near the large orange buoy that marked the top end of the anchor line. Fifteen minutes later the two divers surfaced and gave the universally recognized signal that all was well – a circle formed by the thumb and index finger. The boat swung around to pick them up, arriving at Sotis first. He took off his fins and climbed up the dive ladder. Stewart was only a few feet behind him, by all accounts floating near the back of the boat. But when Sotis climbed into the boat's cockpit, all hell broke loose. His wife said something to him and he suddenly seemed confused, unresponsive. By some accounts he collapsed on the deck; others suggest that he sat down and just didn't move, stared vacantly into the distance. Claudia, a physician, immediately went to work – trying to take his vital signs. Bobby Steele, the mate, grabbed the emergency oxygen bottle and he and Claudia placed a mask over Sotis' mouth. One witness says Sotis was fighting back as the two tried to remove his dry suit for a complete examination. Within minutes they had him settled. Claudia said she was focused on making sure there was nothing constricting his breathing and was trying get Peter's dry suit off to see whether he had any signs of decompression sickness. At this point less than three minutes had passed since the two divers had surfaced. Everyone seemed focused on the emergency on board the boat, though later, Dave Wilkerson would claim he was busy trying to get the boat closer to Stewart. At this point someone thought to look for Stewart. His friend Brock Cahill looked over the stern of the boat and said, "Where's Rob?" The sea was empty.

CHAPTER 1

It was the first day of February – a bleak, cold, mostly grey time of year in Toronto. This year the winter was proving to be particularly distasteful, with temperatures often plunging down to minus 20 Celsius. I hoped that February might pass quickly. Once March arrived it was only a short sprint heading towards spring. There was a bright spot in the day. The weather forecast was calling for temperatures just below zero. If they were right, I'd be able to get out and do some scuba diving in Lake Ontario on the weekend. Now when I tell people that I dive all year around in Toronto, they often look at me as if I'm some kind of fanatic, possibly mentally unstable. But as crazy as diving during an Ontario winter may sound, it's not that uncomfortable in what's called a dry suit. The suit keeps out the water and I just layer up underneath. Though I may look a little like the Michelin Man, I'm actually pretty toasty warm in the water. The only part of my body that really gets cold is my hands. In really cold water – say around one or two degrees Celsius – they start to freeze after 30 minutes, and after 40, it becomes hard to use them. Now, diving in the winter takes on a whole new complexion once temperatures start to hit minus ten. The water is not the problem; it's getting in and out of the water. That process becomes precarious if not downright dangerous – zippers and connectors freeze solid and hands become numb trying to get out of your gear. But as long as it's around the zero mark, this isn't a problem. So the weekend was supposed to be warmish. Maybe Chris and I would be able to go diving. I have to take advantage of these small windows or I spend the whole winter waiting for a chance to travel somewhere warm to dive.

That morning I was writing a piece for a diving magazine. My brief reverie about the weekend had been a convenient way to procrastinate – a common behaviour when I'm not getting anywhere with my work. Continuing the behaviour, I flipped over to one of my favourite online news sources and began scrolling through the stories. Mostly the usual drivel, but one story caught my eye immediately: "*Environmentalist, film maker Rob Stewart missing off the Florida Keys.*" I scanned the article and discovered that Stewart had been diving and filming sharks on a wreck called the *Queen of Nassau* eight kilometres off the coast of an island called Islamorada. At this point he was listed as "missing." The story grabbed my attention immediately. It connected with two of my life's passions – journalism and diving. I've worked as a journalist for the past 35 years. Most of that time my career has been spent as an investigative journalist for some of Canada's top newsmagazine shows – *W5*, *Marketplace* – and I've freelanced for the top newspapers, the *Toronto Star*, the *Globe and Mail*. I also teach at Ryerson University in the journalism department – a course on how to research. I've broken stories that have had national and international repercussions. I have a passion for investigative journalism and I've had some fair success at it. As you've probably gathered by now, I'm also a fanatical scuba diver. I hold multiple certifications, including what are called technical certifications – essentially, training that allows me to dive deeper and longer – ones that require decompression stops to get back to the surface. I'm trained as a cave diver. That's a form of diving that requires a great deal of precision. After all, when you're several hundred metres into an underwater cave and something goes wrong, you have to know what you're doing to survive, you just can't swim to the surface. Any diving-related stories always catch my eye.

So I was particularly interested in what was happening to Rob Stewart. There wasn't much solid information to be had. The initial reports online were short on details and long on drama. The facts seemed contradictory. A few reports tended to suffer from hyperbole. Once the so-called mainstream media picked up the story, the reports became even more confusing. Understandably, it's not uncommon that reporters who know little about the topic are assigned to cover stories. So now the coverage began to include reports about diving tanks filled with oxygen (they're usually filled with air) and how divers faced life-threatening situations as they descended to the deep, dark depths (it's surfacing that's the problem). Regardless, I could still glean some information from the bubbling information stream online. I took the few details that were available, and just out of curiosity I began to do a little research of my own.

I knew Stewart and his fellow divers had been diving on a wreck called the *Queen of Nassau*. I found out that the wreck was a very advanced dive – 230 feet to the bottom. That's way below my capability as a diver. I'm only certified to dive to 160 feet. To safely descend below that depth divers have to start breathing what's called trimix – a mixture of oxygen, nitrogen and helium. The helium replaces some of the nitrogen. Nitrogen is a problem for divers. It seeps into your bloodstream under pressure and when you surface, if you're not careful, the nitrogen forms bubbles in your blood or tissues. If those bubbles form too quickly your blood virtually boils. Think about shaking up a pop bottle and then opening it up. If you open it up slowly, no problem. If you open it up quickly, it boils over and sprays pop all over the place. That's a visual image of what happens if you surface too quickly. Those bubbles will careen around the body and cause all kinds of havoc – potentially stopping your heart, causing a stroke if they get into your brain or clogging up your lungs. Nitrogen is also somewhat poisonous and can cause what's called nitrogen narcosis. It used to be called "rapture of the deep," and all kinds of myths surrounded the concept – divers taking out their regulators and giving them to fish, for example. That's mostly nonsense, but nitrogen does cause confusion, a sense of disorientation and even euphoria. In extreme cases it can cause hallucinations. So divers at extreme depth lower their risk by replacing some of the nitrogen in the gas they breathe with helium. That's an inert gas that doesn't cause as many problems. Divers at that extreme depth *also* reduce the amount of oxygen they breathe. That's because oxygen becomes toxic at a certain depth. If you reduce the oxygen in your gas mix, you still have enough to sustain life and it doesn't poison you. Of course gas mixes are much more complicated than that, but that's the Coles Notes version. What all that means is that if Stewart and his buddies were diving the *Queen of Nassau*, then I knew they had to be using mixed gases, and that process can be very tricky.

I also discovered that Stewart was using a rebreather. That's an advanced form of diving technology that I knew little about. I did know enough to be able to separate fact from fiction in the daily reports that were coming out of Florida. Reporters were describing the rebreather as a killing machine, an apparatus that could go wrong at any second and kill a diver without warning. That seemed a little far-fetched. I'd been around rebreathers and knew the basic principles. I knew they could be amazing instruments when used properly, enabling divers to go where conventional scuba wouldn't allow. I'd been a little jealous when I was cave diving, watching rebreather divers explore the tunnels. I'd have to turn my dive around a few hundred metres in as my air started getting low. While I was heading back, rebreather divers would be disappearing into the deeper parts of the cave. While my dive might last 40 or 50 minutes, they'd be gone for hours. But like any sophisticated piece of machinery, rebreathers could be demanding at times. You had to keep track of a lot of information all at once. If you didn't, then you could get into trouble. I'd also been told that when things went wrong with a rebreather, they went very wrong. A malfunction, though rare, might cause a diver to breathe a toxic mix and never be aware of it. Once I knew how deep Stewart dived and what technology he employed, I started to wonder about why he was diving that deep for filming. I reasoned that he'd have to have a pretty compelling reason to push the limits of technical diving to that extent. I was definitely hooked on the story, and I started to push a little harder on my research.

I still hoped that Rob Stewart would be found alive. The Coast Guard had mounted a massive search of the waters around the Keys. Early reports stated that he had drifted away from the dive boat in the confusion caused by another diver having an accident. During the next three days I watched the news intently for more information. Numerous celebrities had offered services. Family and friends of Stewart were flooding into the area to help. An online campaign to coordinate search efforts had begun. David Goodhue is a reporter for the *Miami Herald* and flkeysnews.com. He's a tall man with dark curly hair – good looking and affable, easygoing. He's worked the Florida Keys for 15 years. He says he loves the laid-back attitude that pervades the chain of islands. I'm sure the great weather doesn't hurt. Most of his work involves covering local stories – fishing championships, small crime stories at the courts and the odd wacky "Florida man" kind of item. The Rob Stewart story was a whole other level of reporting for David. He described the search as the biggest he'd ever seen while working on the islands, "the three days in between finding out that he was missing and when he was found, it was just a massive search, an international search. We heard that Jimmy Buffett was sending planes; Richard Branson was sending planes.... Anyone who had a plane ... was searching for him. I mean anyone with a boat was searching for him." The search came to an abrupt end after three days. On February 3, Stewart's body was found on the bottom, only a few feet from where he had been last seen. The discovery echoed out from the Keys like a sonic shock wave. Many had clung to the hope that he was still alive, drifting around at sea. The confirmation of his death killed that hope and sent thousands into mourning.

I was saddened by the loss. I didn't know Stewart personally, but I was in awe of what he had done almost single-handedly to fight against the extinction of sharks. The practice of finning was killing millions of sharks every year – mostly for the soup trade in China. Fishermen would cut off the fins and throw the still-living shark into the water to die. It was a hideous practice and Stewart was the champion who'd brought this to the world's attention. I'd seen the impact of finning while diving around the world. Sharks had disappeared from the oceans. Twenty years ago seeing a shark was a common occurrence; now it was a rare sight. It was no exaggeration to say that the oceans of the world were emptying of this magnificent apex predator until Stewart came along. I knew we all owed him a tremendous debt. Brian Stewart, Rob's father, spoke about his son's devotion to saving the oceans during a press conference in Miami: "The hardest part about this is knowing what Rob's mission was, what his dreams were, and his plans, and all the things he was trying to accomplish, like showing how beautiful the oceans can be and how beautiful under sea life is…. He wanted to teach people that the oceans are a fantastic place." Rob Stewart had that rare combination of the courage to pursue a goal regardless of the cost, and the commitment of a heat-seeking missile to make sure he never deviated from his objective. Men like Stewart do not come along very often in history, and in my opinion his work as an environmentalist could not be easily replaced. Sandy Stewart, Rob's mother, said "he always understood that if people could see the underwater world, if they could see the beauty in the underwater world, they would want to save it and they would work to protect it, and that is what his mission was, to protect the sharks and all of the creatures, and the oceans in general, because we need the oceans to survive."

There was a worldwide reaction to Stewart's death. His memorial service was held in one of Toronto's larges churches. Brian Stewart explained, "We got the biggest church we could in the centre of the city of Toronto.…

We had 1,250 people crowded in the church, then they brought in extra chairs, and they had people in the street, and then we had almost 60,000 people who watched the funeral online.... He touched people from all over the world. We're getting emails from every country in the world right now ... wishing that Rob didn't die, and saying they're going to continue his mission." Every major network in Canada covered the funeral, and feeds were sent to some networks in the United States and around the world. Guest celebrities spoke at Stewart's service. Former MuchMusic, CNN and CBC host George Stroumboulopoulos was one of the keynote speakers, saying, "We should be thankful that in this little galaxy of stars that our life is ... we had a sun like Rob at the centre of it." Stewart's parents vowed to continue his work and complete the film that he had partly shot. The message given by family and friends was one of hope – a wish to continue to fight to save the oceans. It was a noble tribute to a great man. But after the funeral a wave of vitriol seemed to build around the whole matter.

It began with the bloggers, particularly one called Wildlife Roundup, a video blog posted by a group called Earthrace Conservation and hosted by Pete Bethune. They put up an episode called "The Man Behind Stewart's Death" that essentially accused Peter Sotis of killing Stewart. Bethune confidently stated, "The death of Rob Stewart lies firmly on the flippers of Peter Sotis." Among other inflammatory statements, Bethune accused Sotis of being "a convicted felon who's gone to ground," suggesting somehow that Sotis was in hiding in the aftermath of the accident. In fact, Sotis was still running his dive business in Fort Lauderdale. Bethune also accused Sotis' company, Add Helium, of "selling rebreathers to Libyan terrorists." The narration on that part of the blog was accompanied by pictures of violent warfare somewhere in the Middle East, implying that these were the people Sotis was selling to. Bethune also said Sotis was selling "false certificates on cheap Chinese [diving] tanks" – again, suggesting that Sotis was some kind of sleazy operator who cared nothing for other people's lives. And Bethune concluded that this "narrative flies in the face of diving safety" and that Sotis "failed in his duty of care" with Stewart.

Anyone watching Bethune's blog – it was still online when I last checked – would have been convinced that there was no question Stewart's death was directly caused by Sotis' negligence. Feeding on those kinds of reports, social media began to swirl with accusations that Stewart's "dive instructor" Peter Sotis had been negligent; that the skipper and the mate on the dive boat had been negligent; that Stewart had died needlessly. Certainly his parents both made their feelings clear about their son's death. Just a few months after the accident, they launched a civil lawsuit against Peter Sotis and Horizon Divers. Their complaint filed in court alleged that "as a direct and proximate cause of Defendant Peter Sotis' negligence ... Rob Stewart, was killed." At the press conference called to announce the lawsuit, Brian Stewart said, "When you have safety divers, which are there specifically to keep an eye on you, because quite honestly, as a filmmaker, when you're shooting underwater, you don't know what's going on around you while you're focused on a certain thing, safety divers are a critical part of that equation, and both Peter and Claudia were safety divers on that dive, and they're not just supposed to watch what's going on, they're supposed to keep an eye on the person that's doing the work." The Stewarts felt the same way about Horizon Divers, saying, "Even from Horizon Divers' perspective, not having eyes on the water, of a diver, when you're the dive boat operator, that's your responsibility, it's just unimaginable." If a person believed the Stewarts' complaint, the case seemed to be open and shut: Peter Sotis and Horizon Divers were negligent; Rob Stewart, a neophyte rebreather diver, was lured into pushing himself beyond his limits and died in a tragic and senseless accident when the people who were supposed to care for him failed to do their jobs.

But when I looked at those elements, I wasn't sure I believed all or even any of them. I didn't have enough information to go on and I wasn't going to just believe what someone had filed in a civil court case. I did, however, believe that the events surrounding Rob Stewart's death would make a great investigative documentary. Getting to the truth of what happened would be a challenge but could ultimately provide a lot of people with some much-needed answers. I knew there were a lot of so-called "facts" being thrown around online that had little substance. I knew they would all have to be meticulously documented and challenged, which would be an enormous amount of work. But I'd spent my whole career working on those kinds of stories, so as the story gradually faded from the headlines, I started digging in and reviewing any information I could get. The chase was on.

CHAPTER 2

I started my investigation by pushing aside rumour and innuendo. I asked myself, what did I really know? Here's what I thought: Rob Stewart had been filming off the coast of the Florida Keys near an island called Islamorada. He'd been diving using a rebreather. He'd been trying to film sawtooth sharks. He was working with his friend Brock Cahill, who had set up the dive. He'd been working with two safety divers: Peter Sotis and his wife Claudia. The group was working on board a charter boat named *Pisces* owned by Horizon Divers. They had been filming for two days. They had completed four dives over two days. They had not seen any sawtooth sharks. They cancelled a third day of diving. Sotis and Stewart performed a third dive to retrieve the anchor that attached the boat to the wreck. After surfacing from the third dive, Sotis climbed on board the boat and collapsed. Stewart, still in the water, disappeared.

Beyond that, the rest seemed to be speculation about who was to blame – mostly Peter Sotis if you believed what was circulating on the internet. But something bothered me about the existing narrative that put most of the blame on Sotis. In that story, Rob Stewart had been convinced by Peter Sotis to make three deep dives in a single day with equipment he was unfamiliar with, thereby causing his death. Making two dives in a day below 200 feet was challenging. Making three, according to many experts, was reckless. But I'd quickly learned that Stewart was a very experienced diver. He'd been certified since he was a teenager, held an instructor rating and had completed thousands of dives. He also wasn't a complete neophyte on rebreathers. He could be seen in photographs and video in the documentary *Sharkwater* using a rebreather in 2006. So he knew about the technology and had some experience diving with it. I was also told by several of Stewart's friends that he was a man who made up his own mind. He wasn't someone, I was told, who blindly went along with what he was told. In fact, quite the contrary, many described Stewart as a man with an extremely strong will. So why would someone with that strength of character and that level of diving experience go on a deep and possibly dangerous third dive just because he was told to? That didn't make sense to me.

I don't have anywhere near Stewart's experience diving – I've completed a thousand dives – yet I can tell you that I would not allow anyone to tell me to make an unsafe dive or follow unsafe diving practices. I know the consequences of diving blind. In cave diving they're called "trust me" dives, and from the first day of cave training, you're told to never, ever do them. If you don't know the way in, the way out and what's going on during every step of the way, you don't go. I've pulled the plug on cave dives after only five minutes because I didn't think they were going in a direction I was familiar with. None of the other divers in my team batted an eye. The decision was accepted without question. I understand that there can be a lot of pressure to conform, go along with the pack, not ruin everyone else's dive, but when it comes to my life, I'm not going to take chances – nor would any experienced diver. I couldn't see Stewart blindly going along with a dangerous dive just because he was being told to do so. That raised several possibilities that had to be investigated. First, maybe Stewart was reckless and *would* blindly follow someone else on an unsafe dive. Second, maybe Stewart knew the dive was dangerous and just decided to take a chance. Or third, maybe Stewart knew exactly what he was doing and believed the third dive was not pushing any limits. There was another possibility I decided to check out and eliminate if possible. Using what's called open circuit diving (think Jacques Cousteau and the aqualung), I've done two dives to below 150 feet in a single day, albeit with a healthy break in between the dives to allow nitrogen to dissipate. That would be a reasonable limit for open circuit diving. But maybe it was possible, using a rebreather, a device with much greater flexibility in deep diving, to dive to 225 feet three times in a single day. I decided I had to know more about what was possible using a rebreather.

I called my friend Steve Lewis. I first met Steve when I was working on a couple of television pieces for the Discovery Channel. A group of divers had decided to launch an expedition to explore the Bell Island Mines in Newfoundland. Bell Island sits in the middle of Conception Bay. These iron ore mines had been shut down in the mid-1960s. The owners, so the story goes, thought the mines were not making money, so they waited for the men to take their Christmas break, declared the mine closed, turned off the pumps that kept the water out and allowed the entire mine to flood. They never opened up again. As the water rose on tens of kilometres of tunnels, everything in the mine the workers had left behind was slowly covered in icy cold water – trapping thousands of artifacts in a kind of underwater museum – machinery, clothing, lunch boxes, shoes, people's pipes; the place was like a piece of amber that had entrapped an insect, acting to keep a slice of history perfectly preserved. Exploring these mines is not what you would call a safe expedition. Five years earlier many of this same group had attempted the venture, and that had ended badly. One of the divers died in the underwater tunnels. The expedition was shut down. The museum that owned the mine forbid any more diving. But after years the group convinced the museum that lessons had been learned, better divers enlisted and a strong support team put in place, so the museum relented. I was invited to film the expedition and direct a couple of pieces for the Discovery Channel. Steve Lewis was one of two lead divers. An expat Brit, Lewis is a kind of rebreather diving guru. A long-time instructor with TDI (Technical Diving International), a member of the Canadian Geographical Society and currently the director of dive training for RAID (Rebreather Association of International Divers), Lewis has been diving with rebreathers for decades. He's written books about the subject. Throughout the week of the expedition, I watched and filmed him and the others as they systematically explored these difficult and potentially deadly flooded shafts. I gained a real appreciation of Steve's skill level. So now, when I felt I needed to know more about rebreathers and really deep diving, I thought he was "go to" guy.

I set up a phone call. My first question to Steve: Are rebreathers really as dangerous as some people believe? When I was talking with famed environmentalist and long-time Stewart friend Paul Watson, he'd told me that the minute he heard Stewart was diving with a rebreather, he knew he was dead. "I knew he couldn't have survived … because I knew he was using a rebreather and I knew that he had disappeared and there's only one thing that could have caused that, and that was … the fact that it had failed, that the rebreather had failed.… A rebreather kills you before you even know you're in trouble. There's no possible way he could have survived." Watson wasn't the only one who felt that way. Among my diving friends there seemed to be a general belief that these machines were twitchy and prone to catastrophic failure. But Lewis took a more balanced approach to the technology. He acknowledged they could be dangerous if they were used incorrectly, but he insisted, "There are some things you can only do on a rebreather, that's the whole reason for them to exist. If you want to take photographs of critters in the sea, being on a rebreather is terrific because it's more silent, so you can sneak up on animals and they don't look at you in quite the same way as when you've got bubbles coming out because that noise underwater is quite loud." He also added, "Very deep dives, very complex dives are usually better off done on a rebreather than done on traditional Jacques Cousteau open circuit." But in the next breath, he also warned me that rebreathers can be treacherous: "One of the things on open circuit, traditional scuba, where you've got a regulator in your mouth, you breathe in, you breathe out, you see bubbles coming out, if you can breathe in, everything's cool. But on a rebreather, there are circumstances where you can keep breathing but what you're breathing, you shouldn't be breathing. It either has too much oxygen in it, not enough oxygen in it. In other words, it could be something that's gonna hurt you and you don't know it." He went on to explain that a rebreather is effective for diving deep because it allows you to vary the richness of the oxygen you're inhaling. You want less oxygen when you go deeper – oxygen gets poisonous at certain concentrations under pressure – and more when you're closer to the surface to make your decompression times shorter. You have to be constantly watching that mix to stay safe. A mix of 100 per cent oxygen at 20 feet is perfect to flush out your system after a deep dive. That same concentration is poisonous below 20 feet. A mix of 10 per cent oxygen is great at 100 feet, but back at 20 feet it's not rich enough for the human body to survive.

On balance, Lewis said that if you know what you're doing and you don't cut corners then rebreathers are a superior way to dive. So as long as Stewart and his companions were following the rules and diving their rebreathers properly, there was no reason that the technology should have caused their deaths, unless there was a mechanical failure. Lewis then added that it was theoretically possible to do three extremely deep dives in a single day, but he wasn't sure it was reasonable – for a number of reasons. First, Lewis told me about the psychological affects of diving that deep: "If you walk down Yonge Street, for instance, and you look at a skyscraper or an office building, you look at 22 storeys above your head and you imagine that's water between you and something you can breathe without some special apparatus – 22 storeys is a long way down." The math is simple, Lewis explained: "How far you are from the surface will add a certain element of mental stress to you. If you can stand up in the water and put your nose out and breathe fresh air, you're not deep, but any deeper than that, you start to get deep … so there's that aspect of it, the physical separation from the surface."

I understand what Lewis is talking about. When I dive really deep, I'm always aware it's a long way back to the surface. I don't obsess about it, but I'm aware of it, and I run my dives much more conservatively when I'm down deep. I asked Lewis whether it takes any particular skill to make dives that deep and he responded rather glibly, "The classic is, anyone can get down to 200 feet, 230, I can take anyone to 300 feet; it's not going down that's important, it's coming back up. And the deeper you go, the more complicated it is to get back up." Lewis believed that the kind of diving that Stewart was involved in was on the extreme end of the diving scale. Stewart's parents didn't seem to have an appreciation for that when they described their son's accident at their Miami press conference. Brian Stewart suggested, "Diving can be a very safe sport if you're trained properly, you follow the rules, you check your equipment, and there's a process you go through before you get in the water and part of that, anybody who goes on *recreational diving* is going to expect the dive operator, who's giving you or supplying the tanks … and supplying that service, to have the right staff on board to keep an eye on the divers in the water." The key phrase in that statement being "recreational diving." Brian Stewart was describing a typical recreational diving charter that might take place anywhere in the world. He's right, of course. As a recreational diver you expect the operator to supply equipment and services that meet accepted safety standards. You expect them to have a trained crew that can meet your needs within the limits of recreational diving. But most recreational divers are held to a maximum depth of 130 feet. The first level of technical diving allows you to dive down to 160 feet. Stewart was operating at 225 feet, way beyond any regular kind of diving. Lewis told me, "I would not do three dives sub-200 feet, sub-60 metres, in one day. Physically … I'm not sure I'm up to the challenge, I mean I'm in good shape for my age, certainly, but it drains, takes a lot from you, diving in water that's calm, but if you add in other factors like cold, currents, visibility, then these all add to the stress of being underwater. And doing one dive, yup, doing two dives, if we have to, doing three dives, not for me." Yet Stewart had chosen or agreed to do a third dive on the final day of his film charter. Already I was beginning to see that the accepted narrative being presented didn't quite hold up to closer examination.

Lewis continued his assessment of Stewart's final day of diving:

> I'd like to know the reasons for doing that because there'd have to be … a bloody good reason to do that because it's just beyond best practice…. It's like seeing a hornet's nest in a tree and getting a long stick and saying, I wonder what will happen if I poke this? And poking it and then not just poking it once but poking it three times…. There has to have been a good reason. I just don't know what that reason is. Because normally, I think most of the people you would ask, would say … no, I wouldn't do that. I certainly wouldn't do it.

Lewis raised another red flag about the dives. Apparently, Stewart and the other divers had reprogrammed their computers to allow themselves to get to the surface more quickly. Lewis believes that was folly: "When you start to reprogram a computer and play around with ascent speeds or the gases you've got in the computer, what you're essentially doing is you're conducting an experiment in decompression theory, you're a guinea pig now." Stewart's parents suggested in their court case that the reprogramming was all Sotis' idea. They claimed that their son just went along with the reprogramming, doing what he was told to do. While that didn't sound like the kind of person that Stewart's friends described, it was possible.

Lewis ended our first conversation by suggesting that I contact dive researcher Neal Pollock. If anyone could tell me about the impact of diving that deep that many times, Lewis thought Pollock was that guy. He'd been another member of the Bell Island Mine Quest dive expedition in Newfoundland. Pollock, currently the head of hyperbaric medicine and the diving research program at Laval University, was formerly a leading researcher at Duke University and the Divers Alert Network. He is arguably one of the world's leading experts on decompression diving. Certainly, NASA thought so when they commissioned him to conduct experiments for their space walking program. (Astronauts have to decompress after a spacewalk because the pressure in their suits is different from the pressure in the space station.) That's what Pollock had been doing on Bell Island – working for NASA, researching whether divers under extreme stress produced any precursors in their blood that might indicate an impending decompression hit. When I spoke with Pollock, he was familiar with the Stewart case. An investigator working for a lawyer involved in the case had contacted him for his opinion. His first reaction: these divers were pushing the envelope and it wasn't hard to predict that something critical was going to occur. "If you do a really fast ascent, all the way up to the surface, you push it and you shave off time and you lie to your computer about how much inert gas you have, you're really playing craps and you're not giving yourself enough stop time in the shallow or shallow-intermediate waters to clear out those fast tissues. So the result is you hit the surface and you get these symptoms." Pollock said that Stewart and his partner were diving beyond the knowledge of what science has tested. He stated that for a single day of diving "we have no data on two dives to 200 feet, let alone three dives."

After talking with Pollock and Lewis I was starting to get excited. I could already see factual holes appearing in the accepted narrative. Most media stories had concentrated on the tragic loss of Rob Stewart and offered the simple explanation that Peter Sotis killed him through his negligence. But the story was more complex than that. These divers had been forging ahead into territory that science didn't even have full information about. In a quest to get pictures of rare sharks, Stewart appeared to have pushed the boundaries of diving. At least that's what some of the initial data suggested.

At this point I thought it would be a good idea to talk with Stewart's parents. That turned out to be a challenge. After a couple of email exchanges, I managed to set up a meeting over a drink. My wife and I met them at an outdoor restaurant in north Toronto and spent a very amiable hour with them. They're very smart and charming people but seemed somewhat cautious when I explained that I was a journalist and diver and wanted to do an investigation into what really happened to their son. They agreed to continue talking but made no commitment to provide any information. They also did not agree to give us an interview. Brian Stewart did give me one very good piece of advice. When I asked them about what kind of a person Rob was, he said, "Read his book." He suggested that everything I would need to know about Rob was in that book.

I took Brian Stewart's advice. I ordered up a copy of *Save the Humans* and read it in a couple of days. It was illuminating. Written by ghostwriter but based on Stewart's information, it painted a picture of a man who was infatuated with nature and focused on his goal of saving the planet. From early childhood, Rob Stewart took every opportunity to immerse himself in the natural world. He had such a clear love and passion for nature. The intensity of his determination to protect nature was inspirational at times. But the book also painted a picture of a man who was so focused on accomplishing his goals that he took risks. As a young boy Rob spotted an alligator by the side of a path near his parents' summer retreat in Florida. He crept up to the reptile and launched himself onto its back and pinned it to the ground. He caught the alligator's jaws and made sure it couldn't bite him. He was delighted that he'd caught it. But then a second thought hit him: "I lifted my head and sat up. I didn't know what to do." Having caught an alligator, it was only then that he started thinking about how he might get off the alligator. He eventually figured out a method of escaping unharmed by wiggling backwards off the reptile and making a run for it. A funny story, typical impulsive behaviour for a child, but possibly an early indicator of what I found to be a pattern of such impulsive behaviour.

Later in the book, Stewart talked about a near-death experience he had while filming *Sharkwater*. Towards the end of a deep dive, while running low on air, he spotted a whale shark being attacked by other sharks. His computer was already telling him he had to stop for decompression on his way to the surface and he was low on air. He decided to swim down to the sharks to get a picture. "I immediately kicked as hard as I could against the current to get close enough to film them. It was a stupid, dangerous decision, but it was also the opportunity of a lifetime and all I could think was, 'Okay, my movie's in the shit right now. But if I film this, I'll win awards.'" Stewart lined up a picture and "took what I hoped would be a steadying breath. Nothing came through my regulator – nothing. I had completely exhaled and had nothing in my lungs." Stewart was at more than 90 feet, had a decompress stop to deal with and no air – not even a breath in his lungs. He barely made it to the surface alive.

What I understood when I was finished reading the book was that Stewart wouldn't hesitate to take chances to get the shots that he thought were critical. Paul Watson told me, "I think he certainly had the courage to take, to take those risks. If you believe in something enough, then that just comes naturally. I don't think … you really have to even think about it." I saw my story changing. The narrative of the Svengali-like instructor who led the naïve but idealistic Stewart to his death was not credible. There were a number of other compelling factors at play in the real narrative. I decided two things. First, I had enough information to approach the Canadian Broadcasting Corporation and see if they'd be interested in working with me on an investigative documentary. Second, I was going to try and contact Peter Sotis. I needed to talk to the man the world believed had killed Rob Stewart.

CHAPTER 3

It was a muddy, cold and wet spring in Toronto in 2017, the year I began working on the Stewart investigation. Occasional bouts of snow in late April were depressingly regular. As I looked out of my office window, I only saw the most rudimentary signs of life in my garden – a few small buds vainly trying to break out in bloom. But other than a slightly depressing view, the weather didn't really affect me. When I get stuck into an investigation, I tend to shunt all other concerns to the side. Relatively speaking, I was content. The investigation was going well. I'd been working for nearly three months, spending a lot of time poring over court documents, digging into the history of the main subjects and talking by phone to the people who were most closely associated with the events surrounding the accident. I felt that I was beginning to put some order into the multitude of facts and get some initial ideas about what had actually happened. I was by now convinced that the popular narrative – Sotis leading Rob Stewart to his death – had little credibility. That didn't mean he was completely without blame – I hadn't been able to determine that yet – but I no longer believed the "Svengali" theory.

I had also been working on my pitch to the Canadian Broadcasting Corporation. I felt there was a good story regardless of what the facts finally showed. I submitted a proposal to the CBC's documentary show *POV*. To my delight they gave me a green light for development. In Canada, that's often how the process works. The broadcaster gives the producer/director an initial amount of money that allows them to finish the research and put together a short video that shows visually and thematically what the documentary will be like. If the broadcaster likes what they see, then they green light the full production. That was perfect as far as I was concerned. Now I had some travel money. I could head down to the Florida Keys and meet many of the principal people involved.

Among my first calls was one to the medical examiner, Dr. Thomas Beaver. I'd spoken to him on the phone and he seemed articulate and candid about what he'd found. I'd also been talking to a woman named Linda Kruszka. She'd worked in the local dive industry for 20 years and been pretty forthcoming about what the Keys were like when it came to dealing with diving deaths. Finally, there was a source I wanted to meet who had contacted me through email. He was insisting he remain anonymous, but he claimed to know Peter Sotis very well and said he could tell me things about Sotis that would really put the Stewart accident in a new light. I agreed to his terms, for the time being. I was keen to see where the conversation would go, and besides, I've seen many so-called "off the record" sources suddenly decide they don't mind talking "on the record" after all. Alternatively, he might still give me some information that might lead to other sources, other documents. Either way it was a potential win. Finally I planned to stop by and try to talk with both Peter Sotis and the owner of Horizon Divers, Dan Dawson. I didn't have an appointment with either man, but I'm a firm believer in taking a chance on face-to-face contact. I wasn't planning on jumping out from behind a tree and surprising them with a camera rolling, but you never know what people will say and do when they meet you in person. I'd had one very brief conversation with Sotis and he seemed amenable to talking further. In fact, to my surprise, he didn't balk when I suggested that down the line I'd like to interview him. The only stipulation he'd insisted on was that he'd have to clear any interviews with his lawyer. Fair enough, I thought. I also thought our first chat gave me somewhat of an excuse to drop by his store and offer to buy him a coffee.

In August 2017, I jumped on a plane with cameraman Paul Freer and flew down to Miami. Not unusually for our domestic airline, our flight was eight hours delayed. By the time we arrived, got our equipment and rental car and started driving to our hotel on the island of Marathon, it was well after midnight. Entering the Keys at night for the first time made it a bit of a surreal experience. Not the start of the trip – the freeway from Miami down to the start of the island chain had been typical enough, strip malls and condo developments – but once we crossed over to the island chain, it was like being launched into some kind of alternative world. The ambient light died on either side of the road – very few street lamps – so now we could only see what our headlights illuminated: vague flashes of palm trees, scrubby brush and stretches of swamp. I rolled down the window and breathed deeply. I was met with a blast of heat and then an overpowering odour of sulphur from the swamp water on either side of the road. I couldn't hear anything because of the noise of the wind. This limited sensory experience meant that I couldn't see or feel any sense that we were driving out into the Gulf of Mexico. Eventually I thought I caught the sound of the roar of waves at a couple of points, but it could have been my imagination. Every once in a while we'd cross a causeway – some of them went on for quite a distance. But again that pitch black made it almost impossible to see the water, so again it was a bit like floating though a void. Once we got to Key Largo, that surreal landscape ended and once more we entered into a normal Florida landscape. That pattern repeated – stretches of dark nothingness punctuated by typical towns: Tavernier, Islamorada and Marathon. If I thought the void was surreal, those urban stretches were even more bizarre – alternating between classic Florida strip mall and clusters of tourist attractions with the definite odour of fromage: tiki bars, various "world museums" and "world of" attractions that featured a lot of shells, large statues of crustaceans, massive flags and a lot of brightly coloured plastic. Occasionally we'd pass a marina filled with very expensive boats and signs offering fishing charters. It was like being in the Caribbean and yet somehow it wasn't. I've found much of the Caribbean has a kind of rustic charm. The Keys were like the Caribbean except with much of the charm sucked out of it. We finally made it to our hotel at about two in the morning. We had a 9:00 a.m. meeting set up with Tom Beaver.

When I walked out of the hotel the following morning, the complete flavour of the Keys washed over me. Even at 8:00 a.m. it was hot, 30-plus degrees. It was also already oppressively humid. Paul and I had to load our gear into our van, and within minutes of hefting a few cases my shirt was soaked and I was feeling in need of a second shower. We were going to have to work here for the next four days, and I didn't relish that prospect. But I could finally see the water. It was magnificent, classic turquoise blue, the colour that defines the Caribbean. It was also close by. In places I could have stood and thrown stones in either direction and hit the waves on both sides of the causeway. I could hear the steady rumble of the surf. I thought, this can't be all that bad. Across the road from our hotel was what appeared to be an authentic "tiki" bar complete with a thatched roof, bamboo porch and rattan furniture. I could almost hear the Jimmy Buffett tunes oozing out of the place. By the light of day, it had a certain charm. We decided to check it out that night and have at least one drink, complete with the mandatory umbrella. Beyond the bar, a small marina snuggled up against the coast. It was populated with a mix of local fishing boats and pleasure craft. I could hear the bell-like clanging of the radar reflectors on the masts of the sailing boats. The only element detracting from the scene was the large four-lane highway cutting through the middle of this tropical scene – a busy four-lane highway. Even this early in the morning there was a constant stream of traffic moving up and down the islands.

We set off to meet Beaver. He'd asked us to join him at a roadside restaurant about 15 minutes away from our hotel. When we arrived, Beaver wasn't what I expected. On the phone he'd sounded like a straight-laced medical professional – the kind who wears a suit and tie to work when he's not in his scrubs. Beaver in person looked as if he'd be more at home on a surfboard than in a lab performing an autopsy. With a shock of straw-coloured hair on his head – even in his mid-60s – he looked somewhat like a kid who should be riding a wave and then heading home in his "Woody" listening to the sounds of Jan and Dean or the Beach Boys. But he was warm and friendly with an easy grin and he invited us to pull up a chair. He pressed us to have a coffee and "try the tropical fruit salad." He had just finished a meeting with the lawyers who represented the Stewart family. They were anxious for him to complete his findings and release his report about the cause of death. I was keen to get a copy of that document, but I was equally curious about some cryptic remarks Beaver had made on the phone – remarks that cast a very different light on the case. I wanted him to be clearer about what he was suggesting and I wanted to know whether he would go on the record with those remarks.

If I had any concerns about Beaver being coy, those were immediately put to rest. He wasn't shy about talking and one of the first things he told me was that I wouldn't understand the Stewart case unless I understood the Florida Keys. "People have lived down here for generations and they get this attitude of this is our place and the tourists are welcome to come and spend their money here but that's it.... And anything that would threaten those tourist dollars is immediately assailed." Beaver said that this "Keys first" attitude especially holds when applied to scuba diving, "so the dive community down here is very close knit, and they're very territorial. The money for diving down here is huge. The tourism dollars are huge. And people come down here to basically dive, fish or drink, and there's not really much else to do down here ... and anything that casts the diving community or the dive industry in a negative light is immediately attacked." Beaver added that this "circle the wagons" attitude went well beyond folks lending each other a helping hand. He claimed it extended to a conspiracy of trying to make sure the cause of diving accidents never rested on the operators in the Keys. "Dive fatalities are hushed up.... Nobody wants to talk about them, nobody wants to investigate them, and they're quick to call them diver error or try to throw the diver under the bus, the dead diver, because they wanna protect their industry. Dive shops all know that if their dive shop is sued, then insurance rates for all the dive shops go up. So they're all in this together and all wanna protect their revenue stream and their ... income from these tourist dollars." He told me he'd run into this road block in the past when trying to investigate diving accidents, and he added that when it came time for him to start looking into the Stewart accident, he'd met a huge amount of resistance. "They threw Rob Stewart under the bus from the beginning. The first thing that I got told about him was that he was an inexperienced diver and that he panicked, and he shot to the surface too quickly." Beaver says he looked into Stewart's diving history and found that "in fact, he's not an inexperienced diver, he's a very experienced diver, and there was no indication from his dive profile, from the computer data, that he panicked in any way."

I was a little surprised by the information Beaver laid out for us. It added a whole new angle to the investigation. I hadn't considered that any manipulation of the narrative was intentional. I had put it down to a lack of knowledge among journalists covering the story and a lot of online hysteria. But Beaver suggested a conspiracy to manipulate perception of the events surrounding Stewart's death. I wanted to hear more from Beaver, but he apologized and explained that he'd have to meet with us a little later in the week. He had some work to attend to. He did assure me that he would do a full on-camera interview later and that he had no trouble putting everything he'd said on the record. He also told me he'd be happy to give me a copy of his report once it had been cleared for public release – in a couple of weeks at the latest. In the meantime, he said, if I really wanted to get a sense of how things work in the Keys I should meet with Linda Kruszka. I'd already arranged that meeting, so once Beaver headed out the door I got in touch with her and set up a meeting for the following day. We agreed to meet at a dive shop where she worked.

Paul and I spent the rest of the day picking off shots that we'd eventually need to put together the five-minute demo for the CBC. We found some beautiful out of the way beaches and filmed some classic scenes of families enjoying the water, just being tourists. It was nice to slow down for an afternoon. The previous 24 hours had seemed a little hectic.

The following morning we met Linda Kruszka at a dive shop on Big Pine Key. Of all the islands in the chain, Big Pine may be the closest to what the Keys would have been prior to the massive development that's taken place in recent years. For a start it's still got quite a bit of forest cover. There are deer wandering around the island, several small ponds in which alligators thrive, and an impressive amount of bird life. We met Linda at her shop and she offered to take us diving to a place called Looe Key Sanctuary Preservation Area. I liked Linda right from the start. She was a plainspoken person with the look of someone who spent a lot of time in the outdoors – rugged, tanned and casual. She had long, sandy blond hair and clear brown eyes. She looked like she'd be more comfortable in a pair of sandals, shorts and a T-shirt than a business suit. And yet she told me she'd been a professional accountant who worked the bulk of her career as an auditor for the US federal tax department. She still ran a small accounting firm, taking in only a handful of clients. She told me she'd first met Tom Beaver because he needed an accountant when he took over the medical examiner's office. Eventually, when he realized how extensive her diving credentials were, he'd also hired her to be one of his investigators. Her list of credentials is impressive: a PADI (Professional Association of Diving Instructors) Staff Instructor, certified to teach by SSI (Scuba Schools International), NAUI (National Association of Underwater Instructors) and SDI (Scuba Diving International). She also holds an instructor rating from DAN (Divers Alert Network) and IANTD (International Association of Nitrox and Technical Divers). She holds an additional rating as a PADI technical instructor and a trimix supervisor with IANTD. Kruszka dives both open circuit and with a rebreather. And finally, she also held a 100-ton master's licence to operate a boat. All that is to say, she knew diving, knew boats and knew what could go wrong. In the late 1990s, Linda decided she'd had enough of New York's winters so she retired from her job and moved to the Keys. Aside from her accounting business, she'd worked in dive shops ever since. She said it had taken her 20 years, but by now she knew the culture and the community. But Linda, unlike many people I would meet in the Keys diving industry, was not afraid of a little candour. As Beaver's diving investigator, she knew the Stewart case well. We talked as she helped prep the dive boat for our trip to the local reef.

The first thing Linda told me was that getting to the bottom of what really happened to Rob Stewart was going to be a challenge. She warned me that finding people who would talk wasn't going to be easy. She told me there were families who've lived down here for generations (they're sometimes called Conchs), and according to Linda they like to stick together. "I've been here 20 years and I'm just starting to get inroads to the families that have been here forever." She also explained that the Keys have a bit of an eclectic blend of people. She called it the funnel, "the last place that people can funnel to before they can't go any further." When I asked her what that meant she replied, "It means you get people that are running away from something, whatever it may be. It could be the law, it could be a spouse, it could be kids, it could be responsibility, it could be a job, it could be life in general. It means you get everybody and anybody and you never know who you're going to talk to. You could be one time talking to a homeless person who's a millionaire.... You can talk to somebody who is dressed to the nines and might be living out of his car." It meant people are hard to judge in the Keys. And she added that the Keys have another side – a guarded side: "The Florida Keys, it's a very small world from Key Largo all the way to Key West and ... we are a tourist destination, we like tourists, nothing happens bad in a tourist destination." There aren't many industries in the Keys. Essentially, there's fishing and diving and the tourism infrastructure that goes along with that. "We have water, there's nothing else really to do down here. Fish, dive and drink. That's pretty much it." Anything that threatened those critical industries was something to be defended against. I asked her, "How did Rob Stewart's death hit the Keys?" Linda looked at me as if I'd missed her point and said, "When somebody who's well known, somebody who is down here to actually do his own documentary and publish what he's found … unfortunately [dies] in the pristine blue waters of the Florida Keys, where everybody and anybody can come dive, they would definitely want it to go away." When you looked at the real nature of the Keys, Linda told me, you could see you're going to be in for a tough time on this investigation. "They would probably do anything at their disposal to protect the reputation of the Keys.... They would spin a story to make it look like … it has nothing to do with the Keys or the community or the reputation of the Keys." I made a joke about a television series I've seen called *Bloodline*, a story about the perverse twists and turns in the lives of a long-time family in the Keys and the strange characters and events that populate their lives. To my surprise, Linda said that show really nailed what the Keys are like. Not the answer I'd expected.

By this time we were boarding the dive boat for our trip, and Linda got busy. We didn't connect again until the boat had cleared the channel, made it past the causeway that ran the length of the island and started towards the open water of the Caribbean. Then we got a chance to talk again. Once again I asked her about the Stewart accident. She told me she became involved early on. The night Stewart's body was recovered, Linda said Beaver asked her to come down to the Coast Guard station on Islamorada to help him with any diving questions that might come up. One of her first thoughts was that she was not impressed that Peter Sotis got on the boat first when the accident happened. As an instructor, she told me, she felt she has one overriding responsibility, "to make sure everybody's safe, make sure everybody's on the boat, make sure everything's like it's supposed to be.... This is a dangerous sport." I point out that Sotis claimed he was acting as a safety diver on the film expedition, not as Stewart's instructor. Linda brushed that objection aside. "If it was my student … if it wasn't my student, doesn't matter. Doesn't matter if I was on a recreational dive just for fun. If I'm not the last person out of the water that's not right. It's just a responsibility. When you first become an instructor … you're taught that this is pretty much life and death. So you do want to make sure that everybody is safe. Everybody wants to have a good time, that's what diving is for, but you want to make sure that everybody comes back."

She was also puzzled by the idea that anyone would think it was safe to do repeated dives to the extreme depths Stewart and Sotis operated in – particularly for such a banal reason. "There should have been no reason to do a third bounce dive after two deep dives like that, no reason to do a third bounce dive just to get back an anchor, especially a free-floating anchor. They could have come back for it the next day." And, like Steve Lewis, as an experienced technical diver, she was shocked by the thought that Sotis and Stewart might have adjusted their dive computers to speed up their surfacing. "You're lying to yourself.... That's a huge risk that you're taking and it makes absolutely no sense to do that.... If you do that, you don't know your profile, you don't know what stops you should be making, you don't know the gases that are being absorbed into your body, the nitrogen and the helium, the inert gases and tissues and off gassing, the whole thing has to do with your decompression schedule. You definitely don't want to mess with that."

We reached the dive site and Linda got busy again helping the other people on board get into the water. I'd brought my gear along and I put it on and headed over the side. The reef was in pretty good shape but it was a little tough to enjoy. There was a heavy swell on the surface and because we were only diving in 30 feet of water, that swell was felt down to the bottom. I was blown around quite vigorously and I worked hard not to be thrown against the reef. But it wasn't all bad. At the end of my dive when I hung in the water under the boat doing a safety stop, five large goliath groupers came to check me out. I'd never seen groupers this big before. One of them was the size of a living room couch. They're fairly rare in the Caribbean and these ones were not at all shy about getting close. I have to confess I was a little nervous about having something that could quite easily swallow me whole being that close.

Once I was back on board, Linda and the crew headed the boat for home. As soon as my gear was cleaned and stowed I took one last opportunity to talk with her. I asked her what she thought about the crew on board the boat that Stewart chartered – the *Pisces* – and how they handled the accident. Again she was not impressed. According to the Monroe County Sheriff Report, when Peter Sotis collapsed, deck hand Bobby Steele went to help. Sotis' wife Claudia – a trained physician – also got involved. The captain of the boat tried to reposition the *Pisces* to pick up Stewart. There are differing opinions about whether he asked Brock Cahill, Stewart's friend, to keep an eye on Stewart, who was still in the water. But Linda said either the captain or the mate should have had eyes on Stewart at all times. She said if she were the skipper, "my responsibility is to the vessel and to the people in the water. So I would have had my deck hand take care of the person that's injured.... If there's anybody else on board you get them involved and give them specific instructions, and you as the captain keep your eye on whoever is left in the water. So you get those people back on board. You definitely don't want to leave anybody in the water." Linda believed that safety protocol broke down the day Stewart died. When we got back to the dock and the dive shop, Linda agreed that if I needed a guide to the way the Keys work, she'd be happy to help. She also said if I wanted to interview her, she'd go on the record. But she suggested that when I talked with Beaver again, I should ask him about Noah Cullen.

That evening over a couple of beers, Paul and I talked over what we'd learned during the past two days. Linda and Tom Beaver were clearly telling us there was an undercurrent of opposition in the Keys that might be skewing the facts surrounding the Stewart case. They could be suggesting that the narrative of neophyte diver drowning when led astray by evil teacher might be part of that misinformation. Of course, I noted to Paul, there was also the possibility that we were hearing another form of spin. Maybe Beaver and Linda had a vested interest in casting doubt on the prevailing thinking in Stewart's death. We couldn't completely rule that out. I wasn't sure what their motive would be, but we couldn't disregard it. I thought there was a lot more work to do and a huge amount of cross checking of facts before I could begin to draw any conclusions. Paul, on the other hand, liked Beaver and had a good feeling about Linda. That was worth noting. I've worked with Paul for nearly 20 years on countless investigations. I've learned to put faith in what he thinks and feels. The following day we had another session with Beaver, and we were supposed to meet up with my anonymous source – someone who said he could give us the goods on Peter Sotis.

CHAPTER 4

It was overcast when Paul and I rolled out of the hotel the following morning. That didn't mean it was cooler or less humid: quite the opposite. I could hardly believe it possible, but the humidity had kicked up a notch. It was oppressive – seeming to settle on the body like a blanket of butterscotch – pulling us down like deadweight. It took a lot longer to load up the gear. I made a note to buy a case of water at the first gas station we passed. We'd have to pound water all day if we wanted to work. The concierge at the hotel also offered another friendly reminder – just because it was clouded over didn't mean the sun wouldn't burn. I decided right then that if the project got the green light for full production, I wouldn't come near this place in the summer to do principal photography. But the day took a turn for the better when we arrived at the meeting place that Beaver suggested. He was already at a table at a lovely open-air restaurant that sat right on the water. There was a delicious breeze coming off the gulf, and after sucking back a couple of glasses of ice water, I was feeling much restored. Beaver ordered up a fresh pot of Cuban coffee and a plate of fresh fruit to nibble on. Then he started telling us his story.

He said he wanted to start by giving us a little history. Beaver believed it was a way to put some context into what happened to Rob Stewart. It was a story that suggested that people in the Keys are not above doing things "their way," even if it means ignoring requests from a medical examiner. And bear in mind, Beaver said, "when I say *request*, I mean a legally binding order based in Florida Law. I'm the only person who has the right to order a body to be moved." Beaver contended that right from the start of the Stewart investigation, he ran into a lot of interference. He wanted to make sure everything was being done by the book. It wasn't. Beaver said that didn't totally surprise him because it had happened before.

He told us the story of Noah Cullen. Cullen was a 24-year-old from Key Largo. He loved scuba diving, spear fishing and sailing. He was frequently seen out on the reef in his boat hunting fish. On August 4, 2014, he was seen spear fishing off Molasses Reef – about six kilometres southeast of Key Largo. A few hours later a dive boat went by and noticed that his boat – the *Jubilee* – was wallowing in the water, riding very low with the sails flapping. According to police reports, "The captain of the Fantastic II, Justin, stated he saw the sailboat 7 miles east of Molasses Reef GPS coordinates 25.03.0 080.15.0. He reported to USCG the vessel was riding low in the water suggesting the vessel may be taking on water. He also noticed the sail was half way up and all the hatches were closed and the anchor was in the anchor pulpit." According to the police report, the Coast Guard was called, but by the time they arrived they "were unable to locate the sailboat or any person(s) in the area." With the use of a remote-operated vehicle, or ROV, Beaver told us, the boat was later discovered on the bottom of the bay in 280 feet of water. The ROV video showed no sign of any damage to the hull. So Beaver wanted to know what happened.

Beaver felt he had to retrieve the body and determine the cause of death. But some locals insisted that the death was an accident that occurred because of a microburst of weather that hit the boat and sank it. Noah Cullen apparently went down with his ship. Beaver thought those conclusions were nonsense. There were too many facts that didn't add up. First of all, the so-called "storm" that sank the boat was described in the Monroe County Sheriff Report as "inclement weather had settled in the area, producing heavy rain, lightning, and winds up to 25 mph." Twenty-five-mile-an-hour winds didn't seem severe to Beaver – particularly for an experienced sailor like Noah Cullen. Deputy Sheriff Frank Delgado spoke with John Peacock of Quiescence Dive Center, one of the dive company's boat skippers. He described Cullen as a good sailor who "would purposefully sail into breaking waves, as well as proficiently handle the vessel in 6–8 foot seas." Twenty-five-mile-an-hour winds were little more than a stiff breeze, so Beaver wondered how could they damage a seaworthy boat and kill an experienced sailor. And he was also bothered by the conditions of the boat when it was last spotted – sails flapping, forward hatch closed off. If the boat were weathering a storm, why would an experienced sailor like Cullen lock himself in the forward hatch? Why wouldn't he reef his sails, start his engine, get the boat ready for heavy weather?

And there were other still more troubling facts about the case that bothered Beaver. Cullen's mother initially mentioned to the police that he had some friends involved in some illegal activities. Police noted, "Tanya [Cullen's mother] went on to provide other individuals, who she believed had recent suspicious history with Noah. Those individuals follow: Robert "Robbie" Olson and Ilias Angelis: After research, I found both were arrested on 7/31/14, by MCSO on narcotic charges. Additional information indicated Olson and Waldo were involved in a federal investigation ... a couple years ago, involving human smuggling and narcotics." Two of Cullen's friends were drug dealers and suspected human traffickers. The Florida Keys have a history of smuggling that goes back to prohibition: some now reputable families, according to local urban myth, had made their fortunes running rum from the Caribbean islands to the Keys. The chain is a smuggler's paradise, with hundreds of remote islands, beaches, inlets, any number of places where someone running contraband can slide in and not be noticed. That tradition had continued through to this very day, smuggling marijuana, methamphetamines and cocaine. These days one of the most lucrative cargos was people. But this was not a business run by a few folksy and colourful Conchs wearing cargo pants and baseball caps. This was organized crime. So Beaver felt that a connection between drug deals and alleged people smugglers and Cullen needed to be investigated. Maybe Cullen's death was an accident and maybe it wasn't, but he felt it was his job to find out for certain. There was one more anomaly that Beaver noted. Shortly after Cullen went missing, his mother Tanya was contacted by a local bounty hunter named Michael Waldo, who stated that he "was told by [a] DEA Agent that a person named 'Noah' had been involved in a recent drug investigation in Key West and was under the control of the Federal government." That was another red flag for Beaver.

After adding up these anomalies, Beaver finally concluded in his report that "a natural death is out of the question given his young age, no medical issues, otherwise good health and circumstances of death." Beaver wanted the body recovered. He suspected suicide, but his thinking was, what if they found a bullet hole in the skull? What if they found Cullen had been beaten to death? Beaver wanted to rule out that Cullen had been murdered and then his boat sunk to cover up the crime.

Beaver asked Rob Bleser, captain of the local Key Largo Volunteer Fire Department Dive Team, to help. Bleser had already organized one dive to the boat (without Beaver on board) and recovered a piece of Noah Cullen's skin. DNA tests on the sample enabled the Cullen family to prove the body was Noah's. Now the family was allegedly saying they didn't want the body disturbed anymore, suggesting Noah would be happy to have the bottom of the sea as his final resting place. Bleser was unwilling to do the second dive. But Beaver still felt there was more to the case than the community wanted to reveal. He argued with the sheriff about recovering the body, pressing his case that foul play had to be ruled out as the cause of death. He was ultimately stymied. Beaver told me that incident was a foreshadowing of what would happen with the Stewart case. He told me that the same kind of interference that locals imposed on the Noah Cullen case were also imposed on the Stewart accident. Beaver hinted that in fact the problems with Stewart went even further and may have involved tampering with evidence – with the body or equipment Stewart was wearing. Beaver told me he couldn't give me chapter and verse until he'd released his report. What he would say was that he could back up everything he'd said. He suggested that once I saw the documents and video footage related to the Stewart case, it would support his contention that the locals in the Keys had interfered with the case.

As Paul and I got ready to leave, Beaver, once again, promised to give me a full interview for the documentary if I got the go-ahead from the CBC and came back down in a couple of months. Finally, he suggested I file a request under Freedom of Information Act for all evidence that had been submitted to his office on the Stewart case. He told me that in Florida their access laws were all-encompassing and anything he'd used in his investigation would have to be turned over. That advice later provided me with critical pieces of information that helped me crack open my investigation. I wasn't totally satisfied with what I'd got from Beaver, but I had to be patient. He'd been a willing source, and if I respected his timeline I was pretty confident that he'd eventually give me a huge amount of insight into what really happened to Rob Stewart.

Paul and I headed east towards Key Largo for our second meeting of the day – the one with the source who claimed he could provide me with insight into Peter Sotis: insight that would have bearing on the case. He'd agreed to meet, but only on the condition that I kept his name and face out of anything published. Right away that made what he had to say questionable. It was worth taking time to talk to him, to see what I could do to corroborate his "facts." Ultimately, if he was not willing to have his name used or show his face, he'd be of limited value to the documentary. We met up in a park near the centre of Key Largo. Aside from Key West, Key Largo was the closest thing that the Keys had to a town – not really a town, more of a rambling series of houses and business centres that stretch along the Overseas Highway for several kilometres. The downtown was dominated by one major shopping centre and the most enormous dive flag I'd ever seen in my life. It belonged to a huge dive store called Diver Direct. Other than that, the main drag was a carbon copy of virtually any main drag in Florida – same big name stores. Off the main street, there were some rather funky older neighbourhoods. Old, overgrown houses surrounded by lush gardens that gave me a taste of what the Keys must have been like 30 years ago – charming, rustic. Kind of a Humphrey Bogart feel to them, like a set for the 1948 movie *Key Largo*.

In another older neighbourhood, well off the highway, we met our source. He told me he was a former special forces soldier, an expert technical diver and an inventor who'd made millions from his ideas. He said he'd known Sotis for years. He said Sotis was not a pleasant person: "You know a lot of people say that he's a narcissist and he definitely has narcissistic tendencies. I've seen him do things that, as I've stated before, I consider to be appalling." He told me I should check out a case that was currently winding its way through the Broward County Court system. He said it would tell me everything I needed to know about Sotis.

Later that day, I searched the system and found a case between Sotis and a former business partner named Shawn Robotka. It contained some startling allegations – the same ones I'd seen online by the people who accused Sotis of being responsible for Stewart's death. It claimed Sotis was knowingly selling rebreathers to Libyan terrorists: "On August 9, 2016, Sotis wilfully, wantonly and unlawfully allowed the shipment of the rebreathers to the customer in Libya.... Sotis was aware that the customer was a known militant in the region." The complaint also claimed that Sotis dodged the federal authorities when they asked for a meeting about the potential sale: "On August 4, 2016, a meeting took place between Kaizen [Sotis' parent company] and multiple United States government agencies including the United States Department of Commerce and the Department of Homeland Security ... instructing that the shipment was, in fact, unlawful.... Sotis, however, refused and/or otherwise failed to attend such meeting but was again informed afterwards that rebreathers are a controlled item and the government agencies prohibited the sale of such items to Libya either directly or through a third party." Robotka further claimed in his lawsuit that Sotis was knowingly selling diving tanks that he bought from China that were not Department of Transport (DOT) certified: "Sotis has conducted additional wilful, wanton and wrongful activity ... selling non-DOT compliant tanks and, subsequently mislabelling the non-compliant tanks to conceal their non-compliant nature."

I reminded myself that you can put anything in a complaint filed in court. I could claim that aliens had abducted me, borrowed money from and then assured me I would be paid back by the Canadian federal government. I could launch a civil suit and claim the federal government owed me millions. Just because I file that claim doesn't mean it's remotely true. It would have little value until it had been tested and ruled on by the court. I also noted that Shawn Robotka was a former business partner of Peter Sotis and that the main impetus of the lawsuit was a squabble over money. So again I had to rein in my enthusiasm over this court discovery – bitter former business partners might say anything to try and get an edge in court.

Back in Key Largo, my contact left me with a couple of final thoughts. He said Peter "loses his cool, I mean he's definitely considered to be a hothead." He told me about one incident when Sotis allegedly abused an employee: "I mean if you want to use the word sociopath, that's what that was. That was like, for lack of a better way of saying that, that was like the creepy side. Because he smiled, he smiled when he did it. You know he was proud that he could do it." Why did this source think any of this was relevant to the Stewart accident? Because he believed that it was possible that Sotis would save himself before he tried to save Stewart. That had long been one of the ugly suggestions that surfaced in the early days after the accident. This source was convinced Sotis would crawl over another person's body to save his own skin: "It is not beyond Peter's intentions or abilities or even thought process to, to throw another human being to the wayside for his own survival. That's who he is." Some interesting information, to be sure, but again, this was a person who would not reveal his identity, who wanted to snipe from the shadows. I'd check out what he said, but if I couldn't corroborate it, then it was useless.

We finally headed back north towards Fort Lauderdale. On the way out of town, I decided to stop by Horizon Divers and see if the owner, Dan Dawson, was around. He wasn't. I left my card and Paul took some pictures. My final task on this scouting expedition was to try and make contact with Peter Sotis. Much of the story revolved around him. We were flying out of Fort Lauderdale airport, so I thought it was worth taking a chance, drop by Sotis' business, Add Helium. I also needed a couple of exterior shots of the location for the demo. It took a couple of hours to drive north to his shop, but we finally pulled up in front of it. It was located in a nondescript business park in the western part of the city, well away from the coast. Add Helium looked every bit the professional business – a slick sign, a good-sized building, a new dive van parked in the lot – on the surface the operation seemed quite prosperous. When I walked in the front door an impressive number of rebreathers mounted on stands lined the main hallway. It was quite a big shop, with lots of classroom space and several large offices. I was met by one of Sotis' employees, who told me that Peter wasn't in the building. I must have seemed sceptical because he went on to elaborate, saying that Sotis was undergoing back surgery and wouldn't be back in the store for quite some time. I gave him my business card and left.

Interestingly, I got a call from Peter Sotis shortly afterwards. He apologized for not being there when I dropped in but explained that he'd had a minor operation to relieve some chronic back pain. He absolutely guaranteed that when he was up on his feet again he would call and speak to me on the record about what happened that day Stewart died. He said he'd talked with his lawyer and had been given clearance to speak. I asked him if I could record the interview using Skype. He told me that wouldn't be a problem and promised to be in touch in a week. It wasn't everything that I wanted from this trip, but it wasn't a bad start. I'd made a couple of key contacts – Dr. Thomas Beaver and Linda Kruszka – and had a chance to scout the whole area where I would be filming the documentary. I'd found out about what might be a key court case. I'd made initial contact with Peter Sotis, and while a promise was only so many words, something about the tone in his voice made me think he wasn't just stringing me along.

Sure enough, a week after I got back from Florida, I got an email from Peter Sotis setting up a time to talk. I was fairly excited by the prospect. Sotis had not talked to any other journalist. True to his word, on the morning we'd agreed to talk, a Skype call chimed on my computer. He had a talking agenda – clearly he'd been advised to write out the key points that he needed to make. No surprise there, that's usual these days, but on the whole, the conversation was exactly that – a conversation. He answered every question I asked. He just wanted me know a couple of critical pieces of information that represented his perspective. First of all, he told me, all this reporting about Rob Stewart being a neophyte diver with rebreathers was just not true. He told me, "Rob had been diving rebreathers for over 10 years, many people don't know that but ... Rob was very versed on breathing off a rebreather." He also told me there was no mystery to what was really behind this drive to discredit him. It was about finding a quick and easy solution to what happened to Stewart. "At the end of the day, there's an insurance company that's trying to protect themselves, there's a boat that's trying to protect themselves, there's boat owners, boat captains, there are attorneys ... trying to make money." Sotis continued, a little bitter now, saying, "They're all going to say they're doing it for the good of Rob ... and I wish that they would at least be honest enough to admit that they don't give a damn about Rob, they never have, they never will. They are all doing this for money."

These were hard accusations, but not surprising given that they were coming from someone who was at the centre of such a large maelstrom. Again, I took what Sotis was saying with the proverbial grain of salt. He promised me that if I came down to Florida he would give me a complete interview and tell me everything that he remembered from the final dive. It was at the end of our conversation that he said something to me that resonated. In fact, other than Rob Stewart's parents, to this point he was the only person who had mentioned this concern. "Rob's reputation is going to get hurt. Rob's reputation was not beyond reproach, as is no one else's.... So, it's unfortunate for Rob's parents, that they took this course of action because in doing so, they will ultimately, in my opinion, they're gonna end up tarnishing Rob's amazing accomplishments ... even what he could have done after this.... The effect he could have had on the planet, few people could have done and I think that's gonna get lost, and that's unfortunate." Self serving? Possibly, but Sotis sounded genuine. Just before we ended the conversation I asked Sotis why had he talked to me. He said his bottom line was that he believed I was keeping an open mind. He didn't believe that happened with the rest of the media. "I haven't found too many people that will look at things with an unbiased eye … and you're a real spark of hope to me … in a really, really lousy situation, and it really means a lot to me. And I know you're not doing it to be nice…. You're doing it because it appears that you're discovering truth and that gives me more hope." At the end of the call he invited me to come down to Fort Lauderdale and take a course on diving with a rebreather. He claimed it would be critical if I really wanted to understand what had happened to Stewart. I accepted his invitation.

CHAPTER 5

When I returned to Toronto, I decided that in addition to researching the events surrounding Stewart's death, I would also try to get to know a lot more about his life. That turned out to be a little bit of a challenge. Stewart's parents wouldn't give me an interview. When I started contacting his friends, many said they'd been asked by the family not to speak publicly. Fortunately not all of his friends felt constrained, and ultimately several of them spoke to me at length. I also did a thorough search of what had already been written about his life, and of course I rewatched his documentaries and reread his autobiography, *Save the Humans*. One advantage I had was that Stewart hadn't been media shy. There were hours of material to be seen, interviews he'd given with dozens of different journalists – some of them hilariously bad – mostly done by so-called "entertainment journalists." I could almost see Stewart rolling his eyes from time to time when dealing with a particularly stupid question. But a couple of the interviews were intriguing, delved deeply into Stewart's motivation and revealed a lot about his passion and drive. In many ways, I think Rob Stewart was a fascinating person: certainly, a kind of zealot when it came to the natural world, particularly the oceans. From a very early age, Stewart was determined to explore the natural world and, ultimately, to try and save it.

Robert Brian Stewart was born on December 28, 1979, the son of Brian and Sandra Stewart. He grew up in Toronto. The family was well-to-do and ran a publishing and promotional business that worked with the film industry, the Tribute Entertainment Media Group. From an early age, Stewart was fascinated with other living creatures: "As soon as I could walk, I wanted to be outside catching dragons, or at least butterflies and grasshoppers, and lifting logs or overturning stones in case there was a toad underneath." He filled his room with aquariums and terrariums and populated them with the animals he found in his backyard and neighbouring fields. He preferred his own company and that of animals, according to his book, because he found other children could be cruel – they teased him for being chubby. While vacationing in Florida and the Caribbean, as a young boy he also discovered the underwater world, exploring the reefs close to the shoreline with a mask and fins, spending hours lying in the water, watching various creatures. At the age of 12, in 1991, Stewart discovered scuba diving. His mother arranged for an instructor from the local police department to come to their backyard pool and teach him how to dive. He gained a certification as an open water diver with PADI (Professional Association of Diving Instructors). He continued training during the ensuing years and eventually certified as an PADI instructor at the age of 18. To say scuba diving opened up an exciting new world for Stewart would be an understatement. He completely fell in love with that world; he couldn't get enough of scuba diving and the chance to interact with the living creatures that inhabited it. People who dived with him all remarked on one thing: he was totally at ease in this world. People used phrases like "fish" and "natural" and "in his element" when they talked about Stewart and diving.

If the natural world and diving were the first two pillars of his life, his next major life influence began when he fell in love with photography. That happened during his teen years, and from all accounts he worked passionately at his new craft and to become an accomplished photographer. His parents owned *Canadian Wildlife* magazine, and Stewart was given the job of principal photographer. It was a moment that marine biologist Chris Harvey-Clark remembered with mixed feelings: "I was a young photographer doing a lot of still photography underwater and I had found a great gig, which was a magazine called *Canadian Wildlife*.... Suddenly, the well went dry. And what happened? *Canadian Wildlife* wasn't taking anything anymore. Well, it turned out *Canadian Wildlife* had been acquired by the Stewart family, and now head photographer and chief bottle washer was Rob Stewart." In hindsight, Harvey-Clark laughs about the situation and believes it was a foundational experience for Stewart. "He was a young guy, like perhaps 20? So handed this fantastic opportunity to basically be a photojournalist for the magazine, including all their underwater photography.... I'm glad that happened because I think it helped to make Rob, really, a great photographer, having this gig."

Stewart began getting photo assignments and travelling around the world to complete them. On a trip to Greenland he met Michael Buckley, whom Stewart described as "the real deal, the guy behind a bunch of Lonely Planet and Brandt guides." Stewart and Buckley hit it off and began a lasting friendship that included a number of trips to shoot pictures in remote parts of Asia. Buckley, somewhat sarcastically, described Stewart as "a party animal" whose "parents set him up with his own magazine." But Buckley also acknowledged that he realized that Stewart "had an eye for photography…. You could tell he was going to do something big." In turn Stewart described Buckley as "an interesting character with a slightly odd and awkward sense of humor." One of the more transformative trips for Stewart was one the two men took to the Galapagos Islands. Stewart described the experience as being the equivalent of going back in time – given the numbers and varieties of creatures. The two men spent some happy weeks on the islands photographing for their respective magazines.

And clearly a seed was planted on that trip. Stewart encountered illegal drift net fishing for the first time. He was horrified by the destruction. He and his fellow passengers on board a small cruise ship decided to pull the nets out of the water. Hundreds of dead sharks and dolphins came out along with the miles of line. That might have been the fourth foundational experience that impacted Stewart and set the stage to make him the driven filmmaker and environmental activist he was to become.

While on that trip Stewart also described how he started taking chances to get better underwater shots. Buckley suggested that "he definitely liked to push the envelope … but he was clearly aware of the risks…. That's how you get results." In his book, Stewart acknowledged that he would skip breathe while underwater. Skip breathing is the practice of holding your breath in between each inhale and exhale. Some people do it to extend the time they can spend underwater. It is absolutely frowned on by every major diving organization in the world, for two reasons: if you fill your lungs with air, hold it and then accidently drift upwards, the air in your lungs will expand and possibly rupture the delicate lung membranes. But even more dangerous is the threat of hypercapnia. When you skip breathe, you're not flushing your lungs on a regular basis. Your body can build up "stale air" rife with carbon dioxide, which can cause you to black out. If you're underwater when that happens, that's a death sentence. Stewart claimed he was doing this to get closer to hammerhead sharks for better shots.

At the same time he was out photographing the world, Stewart was also completing a degree in marine biology at the University of Western Ontario. He would study in the winter and spring, and in the summer he would still travel and shoot pictures. He also spent several months working in Kenya on the Canadian Field Studies in Africa program. Following that, he hooked up with Michael Buckley in Vietnam for another travelling and photography marathon. Buckley believed that by this point, Stewart's non-stop agenda was starting to wear him down: "He passed out at the dinner table one night in Saigon and had to be taken to the hospital." Buckley believed that Stewart had "pushed it too far." After Vietnam, Stewart returned to Canada, but he didn't slow down. He went back to school, finished his degree and continued to shoot photos. In fact, he intensified the pace by taking an interest in a new form of visual art – video photography.

Stewart suggested this new focus was the first step in his latest plan: to make a documentary. The other part of the plan was to see if he could get on board one of Paul Watson's ships. It was the beginning of what would become Stewart's most famous project, *Sharkwater*. In 2002 Stewart approached the Sea Shepherd Society with a request to accompany one of their ships on an expedition. He had an idea that he could turn the expedition into a film. "I had no story structure at that point.... I'd be travelling to some of the most shark-rich waters in the world, including the Galapagos and Cocos Islands.... The working title was *Saving Sharks*." Watson agreed to the plan and Stewart found himself on board the *Ocean Warrior* heading south as part of a patrol to look for fishers poaching in protected waters.

Stewart claimed he was nervous about meeting one of his childhood heroes, Paul Watson – whom he saw as a kind of environmental superhero. Watson barely remembered the first meetings but added that being a little cowed by the captain of a ship isn't unusual. "A lot of people say they are. I don't know really why but I get that from a lot of people who join the ships. I think they have this idea that ship captains are sort of like, you know, like ... Ahab or something." Watson said Stewart blended in well with the rest of the crew: "When he was on board the ship, he never acted like he was spoiled. He got along with everybody just fine, everybody liked him, and I never got this sense that he was a spoiled rich kid, really."

The trip south from Los Angeles to Costa Rica turned into a kind of adrenaline roller coaster ride – as Sea Shepherd voyages often did. (When your intent is to ram other ships, that's a given.) They confronted illegal fisherman, went undercover to get footage of illegal shark finning operations in Costa Rica and outed corrupt authorities. All the time Stewart was filming. In fact, one of the strongest memories that Watson had of the voyage occurred when Costa Rican police boarded the *Ocean Warrior*. "I think the thing that impressed me about Rob there is he kept his camera running all the time the police were trying to do their interrogation. And the police officer, at one point, said [to] get that camera out of his face. He said, am I doing anything wrong? [The policeman] said, well, you can't film me....[Stewart] just wouldn't take his eye off that camera. And so he was ... getting a little bit of abuse from [the policeman] but he didn't put the camera down when they told him to put the camera down." Watson also liked the fact that Stewart wasn't afraid to push the envelope when it came to getting the goods on criminals running an illegal shark finning operation in Costa Rica. "He went out and ... went after where there were some shark fins reported on the roof of this building; they climbed up on top of the roof and got chased away and everything, but he got the footage."

During that expedition, one person who came to know Stewart well was Watson's daughter, Lani Lum. "I was 22, [Stewart] was a year older than me ... and you can't get away from anyone on a boat." Given the age similarity and the proximity, the two were to grow close during the two months the ship spent cruising off the Cocos Islands. In fact Lum claimed that Stewart was "probably the main reason I got certified" as a scuba diver. Lum said she liked Stewart because "he had a confidence you don't find in many men his age.... That was the most impressive thing about him.... He could mingle and chat with anyone." Lum remembered that Stewart "wasn't the fun type of guy 'lets party and have fun'.... He was still very centred, even at a party ... he was earnest." In fact Lum believed that Stewart and her father had a lot in common: "He had a great sense of adventure.... He reminded me of my Dad.... I saw a lot of my father in Rob ... a sense of ego, narcissism.... I would say that about both of them." Lum didn't suggest those qualities, when applied to a good cause, were bad attributes. She said committed people "have to have that … drive to do that." Though she acknowledged it "can seem very selfish…. He would go anywhere that curiosity took him…. [He] may not see it as a sense of adventure … [he] may see it as an obligation." That sense of "obligation" to go anywhere put Stewart's life at risk on several occasions.

As a result of being hospitalized for a severe infection, Stewart became separated from the *Ocean Warrior*. The ship set sail and Stewart had to remain until his treatment was complete. The plan was to catch up with them later in the voyage. So after getting out of hospital, Stewart skipped ahead of the *Ocean Warrior* to rendezvous with the ship in the Galapagos Islands. While there, of course, he continued filming, and once again he showed his lack of fear when it came to taking chances for great shots. He'd gone diving to get pictures of silky sharks. He and his dive buddy were dropped off in an area with a dangerous current. Wanting to get some pictures and unwilling to swim against the current with the rest of the dive group (normal diving protocol on the outbound leg of the dive is to swim against the current, and with the current on the return), the two men instead swam with the current, taking pictures,

> but as soon as we came up, in 6-foot swells, we knew we were in serious trouble. I'd never surfaced so far away from the island before. At first I was struck by the strangeness of seeing it from such a distance and perspective, that experience was serene compared to the realization that we couldn't see the boat…. Doug and I had surfaced in the wrong spot, on the other side of the island with the boat nowhere in sight. The initial rush of panic was intense, as everything I knew about getting lost at sea, and how we were going to die, collapsed into my psyche.

The two floated for hours with little hope of being rescued. The current was pushing them out to sea and they were unable to swim against it to reach nearby islands. At the point where Stewart suggested they were exhausted and beginning to suffer from hypothermia, blind luck struck. A boat from another ship just happened to come by and see them. Without that turn of luck they might never have been seen alive again. Stewart summarized his risk taking by saying, "I didn't think twice about the danger when it came to getting footage for the movie. It was just, 'Yes, of course I'm going to do that.' That may seem brave but it's not. When you're going for it, there just isn't another option." Paul Watson agreed that to accomplish great things, you have to be prepared to put your life on the line. "I think he certainly had the courage to take, to take those risks. If you believe in something enough, then that just comes naturally. I don't think, I don't think you really have to even think about it.... I always say that if you're going to accomplish anything in the world, you have to have three virtues, and [they are] passion, courage, and imagination. So I think he was certainly qualified as to having those three virtues."

At the end of the day, Stewart's risk taking and determination paid off. When *Sharkwater* was released in March 2007, it became a massive international success. Stewart became the darling of the red carpet at places like the Toronto International Film Festival and Cannes. The documentary was showered with awards. Virtually single-handedly, Rob Stewart had put the issue of shark finning on the world's radar. There are many who argue that his action saved an entire species. Regardless, it drove a movement that led to the banning of shark finning in dozens of countries and took shark fin soup off menus around the world. Watson believed that "it certainly changed the minds of people all around the world. I get a lot of feedback, you know, messages from people who tell me how much of an impact the film was on their, on them personally. So I don't really know of anybody who's actually contributed that much to raising awareness on sharks that Rob has."

Stewart continued to make documentary films over the next ten years. But his efforts didn't fare as well. He directed a documentary called *Revolution*, released in 2012. In that film, Stewart moved away from the subject of shark finning and instead directed a documentary that looked at how humankind's constant battering of the natural world would eventually lead to our own demise as a species. The film's impact was moderate. His next film project, a short called *The Fight for Bala*, released in 2015, made even less of a blip on the audience radar. In fact, given the impact of those two films, some suggested Stewart was desperate to create another success like *Sharkwater*. Everyone I spoke with assured me it wasn't a matter of keeping his own ego inflated – by all accounts Stewart was not enamoured of the spotlight – but rather to maintain his goal of saving sharks and the oceans. With that in mind, he decided to film a sequel to *Sharkwater*.

Chris Harvey-Clark looks like an affable bear of a man. He's also one of the smartest people I've ever met, filled with an insatiable curiosity that drives him to take on projects ranging from learning how to cast metal statues to stripping a rotting dead blue whale down to the bones just to retrieve the skeleton. He's a marine biologist who researches and teaches at Dalhousie University in Halifax. He's also the university's vet. His primary area of study is sharks. So, in a small country like Canada, it was no surprise that Chris knew Rob Stewart. Chris says he first met Stewart while the two were hosting a celebrity chef event to raise awareness about shark fin soup. "They brought me in to talk about the sort of world ... situation with sharks, and Rob as a speaker about *Sharkwater*, so we were sitting side by side on the podium talking and then side by side at lunch and got to talking about sharks." While Chris says he wasn't an intimate friend of Stewart's, the two did grow closer over the years and spent quite a bit of time together at various conferences and at research locations where their paths crossed. He says his first impression of Stewart was that he was a cautious person. "I would say he was guarded.... He was very cool. He was a watcher and an observer, and he didn't jump in half cocked. He sort of sussed everything out and then would say ... a few comments here and there.... He wasn't exuberant by any means." Over the years their mutual love of sharks brought them closer, according to Harvey-Clark. "Because of my work in Canada with cold water [sharks] Rob was frequently in touch. A couple times of year I would get a call from Rob and he would say, you know, I've got a week off in March, why don't we go ... and dive with ... the Greenland sharks we were studying." Harvey-Clark laughs about the last time Stewart suggested an expedition: "The last time we talked about Greenland sharks he wanted to come out in March. The ice is still on the St. Lawrence at that point in that location. The sharks don't show up until July or August, so I had to explain, well, if we want to do this, we kind of have to go there when the sharks are there.... The other [project] was to come and join me on some of our research work with ... torpedo rays. And unfortunately, neither of those things came to pass. It was always sort of like next summer."

Chris believes that after the startling success of *Sharkwater*, and the relatively mediocre reception of Stewart's other work, Stewart was under a lot of pressure to create something spectacular with his next film.

He says he got a glimpse of this when the two were attending a scientific conference on sharks in Bristol in October 2016.

> I got some inklings into the sort of pressures Rob [felt].... When we were at the [shark] symposium, we hung out a bit together. We went to the Bristol Aquarium ... and he just mentioned in passing that he was still trying to fundraise and it was really hard and he was having a tough time. So I think there was always pressure there. I mean to be one guy, basically, trying to raise funds for a sequel, without a lot of resources – I don't think Rob had a giant team behind him to shake the money tree, I think he was doing it himself, with his own approach, probably a lot of direct approaches to people, and that's a hard way to raise money.

Harvey-Clark ran into Stewart again, a few months after the Bristol conference, in Cape Verde – an island just off the west coast of Africa. "I flew in and within a day or so, I see Rob Stewart in the same restaurant that we're in, and I had not realized that he was going onto [Cape] Verde right after the conference, as we were." Harvey-Clark said it soon became apparent to him that Stewart was not in Cape Verde as a tourist: "We strike up a conversation and he's a little bit guarded about what he's doing, but it's clear he's there on his shark, anti-shark finning mission.... There's a great big, Chinese freezer ship sitting in the harbour and regular traffic to and from it from the local boats and from some of the big boats.... Rob was watching all this. He'd established a watching post in an old fort up on the hill, up behind us, and he was using long lenses and trying to figure who was doing what out there."

Always game for an adventure, Harvey-Clark joined Stewart on one of his undercover operations while on the island. "One day a cruise ship came in and docked, and they had to open the gates to let the tourists off the ship, and lo and behold, it was an opportunity. So we sort of put on our Bermuda shorts and our tourist outfits and me and Rob ... went down there with our cameras and festooned with junk, looking like tourists, and we went for a walkabout on the docks." Harvey-Clark adds, "Rob was really fearless. I mean there was sort of an invisible line where the containers started that was well off the beaten track of how to get to this cruise ship, and as you sort of crossed that invisible line and started to kind of go into that area, it's clear we were off limits and Rob just went right in there like a greyhound down the track." Harvey-Clark says the courage that Stewart showed on the docks was a defining characteristic of his life. "He was not afraid of things, all those things together.... I don't think he courted death but I think he basically was willing to put himself on the line."

But Harvey-Clark also got to see another side of Stewart – a more playful side.:

> I want to tell you one story about Rob.... He didn't let his hair down very much ... but at the same time, I could see where there was a little bit of a puckish nature to this guy. And I think the best example of that was that while we were in Mandello, in Cape Verde, he had somehow bluffed his way onto a little boat that had taken him out to this big, white freezer ship in the harbour. He wanted to get in there and see what was in the holds. And he bluffed his way onto the boat by telling them that he was a marine biologist from Halifax named Chris Harvey-Clark, from Dalhousie University. And he got on there and he got down in the holds and he took pictures of everything, and he came back. And then that night we ran into him in the restaurant, he told me the story, and we both had a really good laugh about that, you know, it was, it was typical of Rob that he would do something like that, I think. He had a, he had a little bit of a mischievous nature.

Ultimately Chris believed that Rob Stewart was a very special person – someone who cannot be replaced easily. "What Rob was able to do was actually appeal at an emotional level and make people care about things, animals, entities that they never cared about before. It's parallel to what Steve Irwin did for creepy crawly, venomous animals and snakes and things like that, but to an even greater extent.... And the other thing he was very successful with is reaching young people.... Everybody who watched his film loved him and loved his message, and more importantly, incorporated it, and people who ordinarily would never have cared about marine ecology or conservation." Ironically, Chris Harvey-Clark would be with the man he so admired at the very moment when the seeds of Stewart's fatal dive were first sown.

CHAPTER 6

Shortly after returning from the Keys, I edited the material I'd gathered into a five-minute demo for the CBC. What I cut together what was ostensibly a mini-version of what I thought the documentary would look like and a preview of what some of the key characters would say. I also wrote up a lengthy research summary of what I'd discovered to that point. There were still a lot of unanswered questions, but the possibility of a good story caught the CBC's attention, because within a few weeks of my submitting the material they got back to me and gave me the green light to proceed into full production. While I was overjoyed at the prospect of being able to complete the documentary, first I had to endure a couple of intense weeks getting all the financing in place. I won't bore you with the details, but I will say it involved the Canadian government and more redundant paperwork than you would believe possible. But at the same time, it also meant that I could start setting up the main shoot in Florida. I now had some money to spend. I could bring some help on board – a production manager to take care of the logistics and, even better, a researcher. I hired Jenny Cowley, a promising young journalist working part-time at the CBC consumer investigation show *Marketplace*. She had done some work for me on my previous documentary and I was impressed with her initiative. Jenny didn't have to be asked to go deeper and follow leads. She did that as a matter of course.

Prior to submitting the demo to CBC, I'd spoken to Peter Sotis, and since he'd not only agreed to do an interview but invited me down to Fort Lauderdale to train on a rebreather, I decided that would be my first shoot. Now, Fort Lauderdale isn't my favorite sunshine destination. I prefer my tropical locations to be more rustic, less suburban. If I'm going to be moving around in temperatures averaging 30 degrees Celsius, I want to do it at a leisurely pace – strolling along in a small town on the island of Roatán, for example, or exploring a jungle walk to a waterfall on Dominica. Fort Lauderdale is a bustling and intense city – part of that megalopolis that stretches from Miami Beach all the way to Boca Raton. It's criss-crossed with a dazzling labyrinth of freeways, dotted with never-ending malls and saturated with condominiums, large wealthy waterfront homes and marinas filled with expensive-looking boats: I'm told it's the yacht capital of the world by one enthusiastic local. Take away the canals and the palm trees and I could be in any suburban neighbourhood in Canada or the United States. It's not somewhere I would choose to spend time, but I was there to work, to finally meet face to face one of the most critical people in my investigation.

Depending on whom you talked with, Sotis was either a "diving ninja" or the incarnation of some evil entity. There were few people who had opinions in the middle. But he was central to the final few days of Rob Stewart's life. He was the man who was Stewart's diving buddy on that final, fatal dive. He was the only person who saw what really happened when they went down to retrieve the anchor. He was also still the main "suspect" in the media and featured prominently in the Stewarts' court action. When the family launched its lawsuit, their lawyer, Michael Haggard, placed a colour chart in the courtroom that described Sotis as an "instructor with a checkered past" and accused him of leading an "absolutely reckless" and "unnecessarily deadly dive."

So, given all the legal and media pressure, I wasn't surprised that Sotis had become shy. He was facing the destruction of his business and a civil lawsuit that could cost him millions. Yet I felt that I had a couple of advantages in persuading him to talk candidly with me. My diving experience had to be a plus. I thought at least he might be comforted by the fact that I understood any technical jargon he might use to explain what had happened. The other advantage I had was that Sotis and I already knew a number of people in common. The cave diving and technical communities are not that big. There may be millions of certified divers around the world, but maybe only 1 per cent of them venture into the world of cave diving. So we both knew people like Steve Lewis and Jill Heinerth. There was, however, one major diving communication problem between the two of us. Sotis was using the language of the rebreather diver. Though I understood in principle what he was talking about, I had no experience with these devices. During our first conversation, Sotis had ended the call by telling me that if I ever wanted to take a course in rebreathers to just let him know. He said he'd be happy to have his chief instructor, Robert Johnson, take care of me. (Sotis wasn't allowed to teach because of a dispute with his certifying agency.) So I decided if I was going to investigate Rob Stewart's death, I needed to really understand rebreathers. I went down to Fort Lauderdale ahead of my crew in order to take the course. That's how I found myself driving through an industrial park in Fort Lauderdale at 7:00 a.m. on February 27, 2018, on my way to take a course. I turned up at the offices of Add Helium and met Peter Sotis for the first time.

It's not hard to understand why some people don't like Peter Sotis. He's an imposing person: not especially tall, but built like a tank. One of his passions is working out at the gym, and it shows. His arms are the size of my legs. He has a massive chest. He looks like he could easily tear most people in half. And yet atop that imposing frame sits an open, friendly face. He has blue eyes and greying, closely cropped hair. He smiles easily and frequently. He's a serious man, but not above cracking the odd joke and taking a little bit of lampooning himself. Within a short time of arriving at Add Helium, I also realized he was an encyclopedia of diving knowledge – particularly about rebreathers. He started using them early in his diving career, and when he founded his dive shop, Add Helium, in 2003, he decided (against all advice) to specialize only in selling rebreathers and giving courses on how to use them. Despite skepticism from the diving industry, he told me, his business model turned out to be a winning formula. One key to his success, he said, was that he went online relatively early. As a result, "I sold a lot of gear online." According to Sotis, by the time Rob Stewart came along, he was selling more than two million dollars worth of gear every year and training more people in rebreathers than any other outlet in Florida.

Before my course got underway with Johnson, Sotis and I sat and talked for an hour. I was a little overwhelmed by the barrage of information about rebreather diving that came my way. Sotis sounded obsessed with diving, it's his entire life – and beyond just knowing about current diving research, Sotis and his partner work with a team of people who try to advance diving theory. It's not the kind of work that cutting-edge research institutions like Duke University were doing, but it was still impressive. Sotis would have preferred to keep the conversation about diving. But I had some other areas of his life I needed to explore. He wasn't afraid to discuss them. I asked him about allegations that have surfaced about an early criminal past. The allegations seemed a little out of context with the man sitting in front of me. He acknowledged that when he was young he'd had some problems.

Sotis told me he was born and raised in Rhode Island. That he had a tough upbringing and left home by the time he was 15 years old. He said he worked three jobs to survive but that he also got involved with organized crime. He described his life at that time as two-sided – he'd work during the day at a regular job like selling cars and then fall in with his criminal colleagues at night. He admitted to selling drugs, pulling insurance scams and to several bank robberies. He described himself as "an angry, pissed-off brawler as a young man." Sotis told me he'd been on a self-destructive tear, a "suicide mission" he believed he "would never recover from." Frankly, he told me, he didn't want to at the time. He eventually found his way down to Naples, Florida, and that's when his life really went off the rails. When he was 27 years old, Sotis entered a jewellery store, along with two other men, on September 5, 1991. They were all wearing masks and they ordered the customers and staff on to the floor at gunpoint, smashed open the cases and made off with approximately $500,000 in jewellery. The three made a run for it but were all rounded up within a few weeks. Sotis pleaded guilty to the charge and served three years in jail. While sitting in a cell in Florida, he said he had lots of time to think things over and he had a sort of epiphany about changing his life:

> There was an exact moment I decided that and I'll never forget it. I was on a second floor balcony outside my cell observing the common area. Grown men were acting like children and I realized that most of them were children in a way. They were uneducated with limited coping skills and no real skills to fit in with the rest of the world, so they had no chance and they never would. I then realized how much I'd sold myself short, how capable I was and I'd thrown it all away because I let my emotions consume me. I was better than this and I ended up in the same place as these other people, so I had no excuse and was a bigger screw-up than they could ever be. So I decided to take on the world again and live up to my ability and prove that I deserved another chance. I

did that and never looked back or made another excuse for myself ever again.

There were some who were sceptical about Sotis' prison conversion, but
regardless of whether you believed what Sotis said, once released, he
turned his life around. He started working in the diving industry, built
up his teaching qualifications and eventually founded Add Helium. At
the same time he founded two of the most popular diving forums online:
Deco Stop and Rebreather World. His life was everything he'd promised
himself it would be. Then he met Rob Stewart in 2016.

Stewart described Peter Sotis as "the greatest guru of rebreathers that
we could find. You dove to 600 feet." Rob had found Add Helium while
making a Google search when he and Cahill were driving north through
Fort Lauderdale. A quick email was sent – could they drop by? Hours
later, Rob Stewart walked into Sotis' store. By this point, Sotis was well
known as the "go to" instructor when it came to rebreathers. In fact,
when the Stewart accident happened and the deputy sheriff was talking
to several people, more of them were familiar with Peter Sotis than Rob
Stewart. Sotis picked up the story from the moment Stewart walked
through his front door along with his friend Brock Cahill. "I didn't recognize him immediately, but they had an interest in rebreathers, they
wanted to know more about them, and the products that we had and
what we had to offer. And it wasn't until partway into the conversation
that he identified that he had done the *Sharkwater* movie." Sotis says he
had watched that movie a number of times and was a huge fan. As the
meeting went on Stewart told him that "they were looking to do another
movie. And that impressed me a lot because … I was well aware of the
effect that movie has had on the entire dive industry, not just the dive
industry but the shark finning industry, and it's affected politics and it's
affected trade deals, it's been a very powerful, it's had a powerful effect
throughout the world. And he did it. So that was pretty impressive."

When asked about his first impression of Stewart, Sotis was surprisingly candid. He said Stewart rubbed him the wrong way. "When somebody calls me dude, it just, it's just not my style. So did I like him at first?
No. Did I respect what he did? Absolutely. He just seemed a little too …
California for me. I don't know how else to put it." Ultimately, Sotis said,
he began to warm up to Stewart. He said he was impressed by his work

ethic once they began training, and ultimately, as he learned more about what Stewart was currently working on, Sotis said he came to admire him. "I consider us friends. But I also think that we both had, we both shared kind of a mutual respect for what both of us were trying to do, and we supported each other the best we could. So I was pleased to have met him and been his friend." Sotis also claimed that it was clear from the start that Stewart already had some familiarity with using rebreathers from his first film. "He was aware of not only their capability, he knew that to shoot the second movie, there were some sharks that were in deeper waters that he was going to want to get to, but more importantly, rebreather technology is silent underwater and doesn't scare away the sharks, or any sea life, for that matter. And he wanted to make sure that he was able to get as close as possible, get the best that he could, and a rebreather was the best way to do that."

Interestingly, if you look at the movie *Sharkwater*, you can see that some of the shots in the movie were taken using a rebreather. In one sequence, Stewart took a self-portrait by turning the camera around and releasing it, so that it sank away from him. It was a great shot and it's quite clear he's wearing a rebreather. You can also see that there are publicity shots for *Sharkwater* in which Stewart is wearing a rebreather. Stewart talked about the experience in his book *Save the Humans*. When he was diving in the Cocos Islands, he said, "Ideally, I would have been using a rebreather at all times.... The only access I had to the pure oxygen necessary to refill a rebreather was when I could arrange a meeting with one of the live-aboard dive boats kind enough to let me mooch theirs. I managed that four or five times." But this time, he explained to Sotis, he wanted to dive much deeper and for much longer, so he had to learn how to use the most advanced models and at depths he'd never worked at before.

Stewart needed to dive below 200 feet. To do that he had to learn how to dive using mixed gases – helium and oxygen mixes. That meant taking several courses from Sotis, learning how to use a rEvo rebreather, learning how to decompression dive with a rebreather and, finally, learning how to use mixed gases for diving to below 200 feet. That was an ambitious training routine, one that usually called for a lot of diving in between each stage in order to drive home what the diver learned. Typically you might do dozens of dives over several months to get accustomed to each level. Stewart and Cahill had more ambitious plans; they wanted it all done in under a year.

Now, I wasn't after anything as ambitious as Rob Stewart had been. I'd arrived in Fort Lauderdale just to take a basic course. I wanted to understand the technology so that when I began to examine the details of the accident, I understood the language. After my conversation with Peter, he handed me over to his chief instructor, Robert Johnson, an easygoing but very capable dive instructor. Day one was all about theory – so much theory that, even with my previous training, I was overwhelmed. First lesson, how did a rebreather work? I kind of knew what the name suggested – it was a device that allowed you to use the air you breathe again and again. I use conventional scuba, also called open circuit. It's called that because when you breathe, you draw a breath from a compressed gas cylinder, and when you exhale, that gas is expelled into the water around you – the breath does not return to be used again, hence it's an open circuit. You can only stay underwater as long as that compressed gas lasts. A rebreather is a totally different animal, as different from conventional scuba diving as flying a jet is from driving a car. A rebreather is a closed circuit system. That means it allows you to take a breath and use it again and again – hence a closed circuit. Once you've taken a breath, you exhale through a hose, and that breath goes through a series of "scrubbers" or filters that will clean out any carbon dioxide. Once the breath has been scrubbed, a small shot of oxygen is added to make up for what your body used the first time you inhaled that breath. Then the breath comes back through another hose and you "re-breathe" it. Now that's a very simple explanation and there are a number of variables that also have to be taken into account when you actually dive with a rebreather, but that's the Coles Notes version. Sotis describes it as "re-using the good stuff, we get rid of the bad, and we replace what our body used. That's what it does, very simply." The fact that you keep using the same breath means you can stay under a very long time.

Once Johnson explained to me how the device worked, he told me there was one critical piece of technical information that I had to understand. I had to constantly monitor the partial pressure of the oxygen that I was breathing. Again, without going into too much geek talk, partial pressure is the amount of pressure that's exerted by each individual gas in the mixture the diver is breathing. At sea level, given that oxygen is 21 per cent of the total mixture of the air we breathe, it accounts for 21 per cent of the partial pressure, or .21 PO2. That's safe for us to breathe, obviously. But as a diver descends that partial pressure changes. At 33 feet, or 10 metres, the pressure on a diver doubles and so oxygen's partial pressure is now doubled to become .42 PO2. At 66 feet, or 20 metres, the pressure has tripled and now the PO2 is .63, and so on, the deeper you go. Well, here's the rub. When oxygen reaches a certain point, 1.16 PO2, it becomes toxic to humans – when you're breathing air that happens at around 180 feet deep. It's not a precise line that you cross and are suddenly afflicted with oxygen toxicity; it's more of an increasing chance of being poisoned once you get below that depth. On the other end of the rebreather scale, if you let your oxygen supply fall below .14 PO2, then your body doesn't have enough oxygen to sustain life. That's called hypoxia. Now, why would a rebreather diver care about this? Johnson explained that when you're diving with a rebreather, in order to maximize your diving time you try to keep the gas you're breathing between .90 PO2 and 1.12 PO2. By doing that, you reduce the amount of time you spend decompressing – the richer the oxygen you breathe, the less nitrogen is being taken into your system, and nitrogen is the gas that creates problems with the bends. Johnston explained that if I didn't pay attention to those levels by monitoring my computer constantly throughout the dive, it would not be all that hard to have the level change suddenly and now you're breathing a toxic mix. It's a bit like riding a bike on a road between two steep cliffs. You're fine if you stay in the middle, but if you veer off in either direction then you're going to be in deep trouble.

Johnson explained to me that after a while all this monitoring and adjusting levels would become second nature to me. He said it was just part of the drill. In fact, over the next four days I was relentlessly drilled by Johnson on this safety issue. He kept me for eight hours of classroom training on the first day, just going over basic diving theory. When we finally got into the pool on day two, he put me though drill after drill where I adjusted my oxygen levels to the right partial pressure, allowed it to go off kilter and then brought it back in line again. He did that by making me shut down my gas supply and breathe off the rebreather until the partial pressure of oxygen dropped. Then he made me turn on my gas again and bring the PO2 back to a safe level. He did this not only to illustrate how important it was to monitor these levels but to show me that if I have some kind of catastrophic gas loss, I've actually got about ten minutes to sort things out – switch to my backup gas. On conventional scuba, that kind of gas loss means you essentially have seconds to sort out the problem before all the gas will drain from the tank.

This shut-off, turn-on drill would be repeated and repeated during the next three days. Shut my gas down, let the PO2 drop, turn it on and bring the PO2 back to a safe level. Johnson also made me practise using my bail-out bottles. These are conventional scuba tanks that were clipped to my side and could be used if the rebreather failed. We did that drill again and again. That part of the training wasn't a big challenge. When I've dived in caves with conventional scuba, I've carried spare air and I've often used it. In total, I spent four hours floating at the bottom of the pool going through various drills. That doesn't include the hours I spent learning how to properly assemble and disassemble the gear. That's a rigorous routine in itself. One of the biggest training challenges was trying to maintain control of my buoyancy. With conventional scuba, when I want to fine-tune my buoyancy I take in a slightly larger or smaller breath. Because I'm drawing compressed gas from a tank, as it expands in my lungs it provides increased buoyancy. You have to be careful not to take in too much gas or rise too much, to avoid hurting your lungs, but it's a standard way of fine-tuning your position in the water. The problem with a rebreather is that when you draw in a breath, you're really just using the same breath that you've been using all along – there's no increase in volume to cause you to rise. The slight bit of oxygen you add is insignificant. So when I took a deep breath at the bottom of the pool, expecting to rise up slightly, nothing happened. I hit the bottom a number of times before I realized that I had to find another way to fine-tune my buoyancy. When I got back to Add Helium at the end of the day to clean my gear, Sotis asked me how it was going. I gave him the brief version of how the day went and asked him if he had a couple of minutes to talk when I was done.

I found him in his office a few minutes later and told him that there was something else I needed to ask about: the allegations in the court action launched by his former partner. The look on his face told me he was sick and tired of explaining this to people, but he took a breath and started to lay out his side of the story. The so-called "Chinese tanks" were not products that were dangerous in the least. He explained that they are one of the options that rEvo, the Belgian company that makes most of his re-breathers, gave to their clients. They are not certified by the Department of Transport (DOT), but are they are certified by an equivalent organization in Europe. He noted that firefighters across North America used a similar kind of carbon composite tank and they have been found safe for many years. He admitted that dive shops in the United States cannot fill these tanks, but they are a viable alternative in other parts of the world.

My next question, about the "terrorist" sale, really offended him. He acknowledged that he did sell rebreathers to a man with an Arabic-sounding name. He claimed the order came from Virginia and that he wasn't about to assume that every person with an Arabic name was a terrorist, even if they were from Libya. He acknowledged that his manager eventually got an email from Special Agent Brent Wagner of the Department of Commerce telling Add Helium that "the reported $100,000 [in] funds from the recent transaction with Mohammad Zaghab were based on an illegal transaction in violation of U.S. Export Laws and the Export Administration Regulation." Sotis claimed that by the time they got that notification, the rebreathers had been shipped to Virginia by the owner and he had no way to bring them back. He said they provided the Department of Commerce with all the paperwork they asked for and he hadn't heard from them since. That was three years ago. I emailed and called Special Agent Wagner, but he'd been transferred out of the Miami office and they wouldn't tell me his new location, nor would they speak about whether there was still an active investigation. I also contacted Special Agent Alan Berkowitz of the Department of Commerce's export enforcement branch to ask about the case, and all he would say was "I'm not at liberty to discuss anything." That statement led me to initially believe that the case was dead – that the agent was doing the usual "won't confirm or deny" but that nothing was happening and Sotis was correct about the Department of Commerce having gone away. A year or so later, those prophetic words "not at liberty to discuss anything" would come back and take on a whole new meaning.

In the meantime, Sotis told me that he believed the "terrorist" investigation was the result of his former business partner, Shawn Robotka, notifying the authorities about the sale after he'd filed his court case. "That entire situation was exaggerated and promoted by Shawn Robotka as the only way a junior partner can unseat a managing partner is they need to show some negligence." According to Sotis, "Robotka could never prove his point and the lawsuit died on the vine." Yet the case was still before the courts. There was no way of knowing whether there was any substance to Robotka's claim, though it was of interest that Robotka's lawyers had recused themselves as counsel from the case a few years earlier – he was now representing himself. Sotis' lawyer also withdrew late in the case, and last I checked the whole matter was still languishing in the courts.

By day three, I was told we were going out diving in the open water off Fort Lauderdale. Needless to say I was a little nervous about the whole prospect. But the following morning seemed to be perfect for diving – bright and sunny. The early morning sun threw a lovely intense tropical light on everything as I drove down from my hotel towards the docks, where I met Johnson and Sotis for my first real rebreather dive. The docks were on the inner canal and the boat was a large sport diving vessel with lots of room for gear. Johnson watched me as I assembled my rebreather and the rest of my gear and loaded it onto the boat. He made a few corrections and then loaded his own gear. The boat pulled out just after 9:00 a.m. and cruised down the inner canal. We made a short turn towards the open water, motored under a highway overpass and then were out on the sea. Sotis explained that we were going to dive on a wreck that was in about 90 feet of water. He told me that Johnson would put me through the same drills that I'd gone through in the pool the day before. We reached the mooring buoy all too soon for me, and I was told to suit up. Johnson was already in his gear and he ran me though my pre-dive checklist. It's extensive. Unlike conventional scuba, where your pre-dive list involved maybe half a dozen items, a rebreather dive involved an extensive checklist – about 30 different steps. This is a must-do before every single dive: one of the most critical steps – pre-breathing on your loop. This involved turning on the rebreather and sitting on the boat breathing with it for a minimum of five minutes. You do this to make sure that it's functioning properly, cleaning out the carbon dioxide and adding new oxygen. You want to make sure there are no leaks in the system and that some kind of toxic mixture caused by water somehow getting into the scrubbing chemicals isn't contaminating the system. If something is going to go wrong, the idea is that it's better to have it go wrong while you're on the boat.

Finally, I was suited up, and along with Johnson and Sotis I headed for the water. With a final deep breath I stepped off the back of the boat and hit the water. I sank down and made my way to the mooring line where Sotis and Johnson were waiting for me. I noticed again that breathing on this machine was very different from breathing on a conventional scuba system. Normally, with conventional scuba, you just breathe in and breathe out as you would on land. But this device required a new approach to breathing. If you breathed in too deeply or too fast, you drained the counter lung and ran out of gas to breathe. If you breathed out too quickly and too deeply, there was nowhere for your breath to go – the counter lung was already full – a bit like breathing out while holding your mouth shut. So I had to find a happy medium – learn to breathe slowly and evenly to allow the gas to flow through the filters. I'd only been submerged for a matter of seconds but Johnson was already pointing at my computers. I hadn't checked the partial pressure of my gas since we'd descended. I looked, and sure enough, it was too high. So I added some gas that's called diluent (carried to dilute the oxygen) and I watched as the PO2 returned to where it should be. Johnson gave me the okay sign, I returned it, and we dropped down the line to the wreck at about 90 feet, or 30 metres, below. It took a bit of adjusting to find my trim and buoyancy, and Johnson seemed well aware that this would be the case. He signalled for me to follow him and we took some time to just swim around the wreck to give me some time to adjust. After about ten minutes he found a flat spot on the deck of the wreck and once again put me through all of the operational and safety drills for a rebreather. He seemed happy when we were done, and once again he signalled that we were going for a little swim around.

Now that I was a little more comfortable with the rebreather, I had a chance to look around. The first thing I noticed as we drifted towards the front of the wreck was that the fish *really* didn't seem to register that I was there – a large puffer fish hanging by the railing paid no attention to me, even when I slowly swam to within a foot. A school of barracuda rocketing around the bow came within inches of me and showed no interest, and in fact really didn't seem to be even aware that I was there. Normally, using scuba, it's hard to get within ten feet of underwater creatures. Though I was still not overly confident, I was feeling a little better as we completed the dive. By the time we'd done a second dive that day (more drills), I was actually feeling pretty good about rebreathers and quite confident that I wasn't going to kill myself.

We spent a second day diving off the coast of Fort Lauderdale, and by the end, as we were motoring back to the shore, I had decided I'd changed my mind about rebreathers. From being uncertain about whether they were accidents just waiting to happen, I'd come to realize that in many ways they were actually safer than conventional scuba. Your ability to control the amount of oxygen you breathe at all times gives you more options; it keeps you safer in some ways. But I also realized they are very precise machines. You cannot be cavalier about how you use them. You have to follow all of the protocols and you have to follow them exactly. If you don't, you can and will run into problems very quickly. I decided that if I were to switch from conventional diving to rebreather diving, it would have to be a total commitment. Either all these safety procedures would have to become "muscle memory" from constant use or I'd run a huge risk of forgetting some critical detail. I didn't believe I could switch part-time.

According to Sotis, Rob Stewart's training went off without a hitch: "I expected Rob to be exceptional in the water and he was. With the amount of experience that he had and just his love for the water, he was just naturally in his element when he was in the water. And he was a phenomenal student. He already had a lot of experience; he had a tremendous amount of comfort. He also was a very intelligent guy, he had a good education and he really enjoyed learning the more sophisticated side to rebreather diving. He wanted to know everything about it." Stewart completed his first course, the introduction to rebreathing, in the summer of 2016. He and Brock then went back to California, and there's some evidence to suggest that he was using his rebreather for diving in the Pacific Ocean. A scene from *Sharkwater Extinction* shows him and Brock using their rEvos. Sotis said, "They were constantly calling me.... Rob would call me from, you just never knew where it was going to come from next, and say, I'm here and where can I get some absorbent for my rebreather. So they were always looking for supplies or they needed some type of piece of equipment overnighted somewhere, because these guys were in the water a lot." In the early fall of 2016, Stewart returned to Add Helium to take a second rebreather course. This one allowed them to go deeper, to 180 feet, or 60 metres. It also taught them how to incorporate decompression stops, significantly increasing their bottom time. Sotis said that just as in the first course, Rob sailed through the second training course with ease.

Finally, in January 2017, they came back for the third course. Once again they were looking to dive deeper – this course would certify them to dive below 300 feet, or 100 metres. For that they needed to be trained in the use of mixed gases – adding helium to the mix to reduce the diver's exposure to nitrogen. Sotis said, "Brock contacted me, and they wanted to come in to complete their full Trimix training and then go and do a shoot down in the Keys and finish off. They knew of some sharks, some very special sharks on a wreck that they wanted to try and film." They completed the course, but they didn't finish the final open water dive required for certification. The weather turned nasty, and they were blown out. Meanwhile, according to Sotis, Stewart and Cahill asked him if he would accompany them on a series of deep dives they wanted to do off the coast of the Florida Keys. There was a wreck there called the *Queen of Nassau*. They'd been told that around that wreck there was a rare congregation of sawtooth sharks. Initially, Sotis said he couldn't help. "My schedule didn't allow for it.... [Stewart] did hire some actual hands and he got some volunteers to assist him, but that trip didn't work out because the weather didn't cooperate." Sotis claimed they approached him a second time to help them out on the dives. In December 2016, Brock Cahill sent an email to Sotis saying, "I don't want to push you on this Peter but it would be a real boost in confidence to have you on the mission. As you can probably guess, we need a superhero, not just a regular Joe Schmo diver, someone who can hot drop on this wreck, tie off, and be a super badass if anything goes awry. You are that guy." This time Sotis' schedule was open. He agreed to go on the dives. It would be a pivotal decision in his life. Sotis says he took no money for his services. He went along as a volunteer safety diver. Yet that act, of what he describes as generosity, would ultimately destroy his reputation and his business and leave him open to a multi-million-dollar lawsuit.

CHAPTER 7

The origins of Rob Stewart's third dive can be found months earlier in
Bristol, England. In October 2016 Stewart attended the annual European
Elasmobranch Association's conference. For the unscientific, that's a
conference about sharks. Marine biologist Chris Harvey-Clark attended
the conference. He said he saw the exact moment that the seeds of the fatal dive were planted: "I can tell you about that pretty much from start to
finish." It began, according to Harvey-Clark, at a lecture by an American
scientist named Dr. Dean Grubbs on sawtooth sharks, or sawfish as
they're sometimes called. For those who haven't seen a sawtooth shark,
they look like a flattened version of a shark, with a long, saw-like bill ex-
tending from their face. This bill is covered in teeth that protrude at right
angles along the length of the bill. The whole appendage looks sort of
like a saw – hence the name sawtooth shark. According to Harvey-Clark,
"Dean Grubbs had been studying smalltooth sawfish and he had heard
from some technical divers about this unusual aggregation of seven or
eight on this wreck, this deep wreck, the *Queen of Nassau.*" That was
special because groups of sharks like that can only mean a few things:
"Not only have you found a rare species but you found an aggregation,
and when you see an aggregation like that, there are generally only two
reasons you see those sort of aggregations, it's either food or sex, either
one of which is extra intriguing. You're not just seeing animals doing
their thing passively, they're actually engaged in a critical part of their
life cycle."

When Stewart heard Grubbs talking about this, Harvey-Clark said,
"His ears just went right up. It was during a coffee break during the meeting and Rob was basically pumping Dean for all the information he could
get." Harvey-Clark believed Stewart might have thought this could be a
critical element for his next documentary, "to be the first one to show a
mating aggregation of sawfish.... There'd be nothing, nothing like that

anybody else had ever done." Here was chance to find a group of rare sharks in relatively clear water and get a shot nobody had ever been able to film. The film director in Rob Stewart must have seen a massive opportunity. Harvey-Clark says, "I watched the change in Rob's expression, I mean he was jubilant after he had … talked to Dean. You could tell he was really excited. And Rob's not the kind of guy who, in my experience of him, you know, doesn't wear his heart on his sleeve, and to see him up and really cranked up about that, you could tell this is really something."

Harvey-Clark says there was a good reason for Stewart to be excited: "The smalltooth sawfish … is endangered, not extinct, but well on that path." What's more, as a species, the sawtooth shark presented some dramatic possibilities for a filmmaker. "I mean for one thing, they're huge. They get up to about 24–25 feet long, which about a fifth is this big bill sticking out off the end of the body, with these teeth.… These are formidable animals." Harvey-Clark added that even the way this species feeds is filmic. "It turns out this long snout they have is studded with electro-receptors and what they're doing is they're swimming around down, probably mostly on the bottom, using that long metal detector on the end of their head to detect fish, and then when they find them, they do a little bit of slice and dice and ingest the fish. So that's the smalltooth sawfish, very interesting, enigmatic species, and not much known about its biology." Harvey-Clark thought the final attraction for Stewart would have been that "scarcely any footage in the wild exists of these, partially because their preferred habitat is estuaries and river mouths and areas where the salinity is kind of mixing and it's turbulent and it's dark."

I called Dean Grubbs in the fall of 2017 and asked him about his interaction with Stewart at the shark conference in Bristol. Grubbs said that when Stewart came over to him he wanted to know it all – when were the sharks there, how deep was the water, how clear was the visibility. Grubbs had no problem sharing, but when Stewart invited him to dive the wreck, Grubbs declined, saying it was too deep for him. Ironically, Grubbs told me his team had dived the wreck just before Stewart arrived in January 2017 and found the fish were no longer hanging around. They had moved up the coast into shallower water. Stewart did not call Grubbs prior to making his dive to check if the fish were still at the *Queen of Nassau*. But in Brock Cahill's court deposition he says they had a number of reasons they were really counting on finding sawtooths on the wreck. They'd already tried to find the fish once in the Bahamas and had "struck out at Andros." The *Queen of Nassau* may have represented their last chance to get the shot for the film. At the beginning of 2016 neither Cahill nor Stewart was certified on rebreathers or trimix diving. In other words neither man had the skills to get the shot. By the beginning of 2017 they'd certified on rebreathers and they were now only one dive short of the certification they needed to reach the sharks of the *Queen of Nassau*. They decided to go ahead with the expedition.

Emails filed in court also showed that it was Cahill who contacted Horizon Divers in Key Largo to arrange the charter. They were a well-regarded business that had lots of experience working with technical divers. In fact their owner, Dan Dawson, was a fully certified technical diver whom Rebreathers USA describes as the "go to technical instructor in the Florida Keys." He holds multiple technical and recreational diving certificates from SDI, TDI and PADI. He also holds a certification from ERDI (Emergency Response Diving International) in public safety diving training. ERDI teaches courses in forensic recovery diving. In a series of emails between Dawson and Cahill the two of them set up the dive with a minimum of fuss. Brock kicked off the emails with a little glad handing, saying, "Your outfit looks to be the authority in this area, and i [sic] sure am optimistic that you can help us make magic!" Cahill and Horizon Divers exchanged emails and little was said about the technical aspect of the diving. At one point *Sharkwater* producer Karen Shaw mentioned in an email, "I'm assuming you also talked to Brock about the fact that they will be diving with rebreathers. I don't know what that means for the boat, but just letting you know." Other than that there's little discussion about the difficulty of such dives. On January 30, 2017, Stewart, Cahill, Peter Sotis and his wife Claudia, along with the crew, boarded the *Pisces* and headed out for their first day of diving on the *Queen of Nassau*.

The world has a unique window into what happened on that first day of diving. That's because a freelance cameraman hired by Stewart shot footage that first day. That footage was given to the medical examiner as part of his investigation. Under Florida law, that became part of the public record. So when I asked the medical examiner for copies of all of his material, he also turned over the footage that he'd used in his investigation. What it showed was a sunny morning in late January, with Cahill, Stewart, Peter Sotis and his wife Claudia Sotis loading the boat – the

Pisces – with their gear. The skipper of the boat, Dave Wilkerson, was hovering in the background. After completing the filming of a sequence of loading the gear, the group sat down in the boat and had the cameraman film their dive planning. Sotis took the lead. The sections of conversation included below are from that video material. Sotis laid out how they would get down to the wreck:

> I thought we'd use a target depth of 200. The wreck sits in about a two and a quarter, 230, so this is going to give us a chance to dive between 170 and two and a quarter with about the same profile.… It's not going to be a long dive, so using 1.3 PO2 at the bottom's good. We've got our diluent at 10/50, but I selected it for that. Okay. And our bailout – when I got into our preferences, I kind of came up with about an average for all of us, I think about .4 is good for all of us. We're going to use a 90/90 GF [gradient factor] with … our bailouts are full. So with that, with an 80% conservatism, what we're looking at is about 65 minute TTS [total time to surface] on the good day mode, when we're diving.

That's a lot of technical jargon, but breaking it down simply, Sotis was telling them the parameters of their dive settings to allow them to spend the maximum time at the bottom. Sotis walked them through how they should set up their dive computers and made sure that nobody had any problems understanding what they were doing. Then he added, "In the event that anything goes wrong, I'm just gonna hand [Stewart] a regulator and we're going straight up. So if we're gone … there was a problem. Okay. So we've got one set of tanks for the two of us and if anything goes wrong I'm just taking him straight up." He added that caveat because Stewart wasn't carrying a bailout bottle while filming. The camera was too large and bulky for him to carry the extra gear. So Sotis agreed to carry his gas for him and stay close enough that Stewart could always access the emergency gas. What's interesting about this was that it added another layer of pressure to the dive. Normally a diver carries his own bailout gas and it's accessible if something goes wrong. In this case Stewart would not have any bailout gas with him. Remember, this was a deep and dangerous dive and one of the primary safety factors was radically modified. There was no question that the group trusted Sotis when it came to planning a series of dives to below 200 feet. Cahill said, "We had confidence in Peter and in our ability to make the dive. We had had experience to greater depths even just in the days previous." In reality, while Sotis had thousands of dives on a rebreather under far deeper and more dangerous conditions – including one dive to below 600 feet – Stewart and Cahill had virtually no experience at that depth. On Stewart's dive computer there was only one dive to that depth logged before they dived the *Queen of Nassau*.

While Sotis took the lead when it came to the diving, it was equally clear who was in charge when it came to their primary mission, filming – Stewart. He laid down the plans on how and where and what they were going to be doing while on the dive if they ran into any sawfish. "We want to get footage of sawfish because, basically, people haven't seen them in a while, in this way before, and there's no footage of them, and they're some of the most endangered sharks in the world. Their populations have dropped way more than 95 per cent because their saw so easily gets caught in nets. So if we have an opportunity to film one of the most endangered sharks in the world and show people the majesty of this animal, we should." Stewart was equally clear about how the crew should behave around the sharks: "Sharks are very afraid of people, particularly sharks like this, that aren't really massive predators. They've got senses all over their body that detect movement, they've got senses that detect electromagnetic fields, so if we're really excited or we're really aggressive, they'll feel that. If our heart rates are moving too fast, they'll feel that. So, when we're ripping around under water, we want to be really calm and move really slowly." And Stewart also decided who was going to be in each dive team. "I think the best way to do it is if we split up into teams, with me and you taking one side of the wreck and you two taking another side of the wreck." Stewart insisted they break into teams and then when one team found a fish, the other team should come and get him and leave him and his dive buddy to film the animal. "We'll work that sawfish for a while, we'll probably be in the sand, and I'll show you some footage before we go so you can recognize the pattern of what it looks like in the sand. I'll work and I'll film that for a while and then if you guys can go and scout and see if you can find another sawfish or groups of sawfish. As soon as you see them, back off." Stewart's instructions even included details about the direction the divers should use when approaching sharks:

With sharks, the worst place to approach a shark from like its blind spot, because they don't really have blind spots, they can still see you and feel you from here, but if you do approach a shark from that direction, it thinks you're trying to sneak up on it. So if you ever approach one of these, you approach them from like the head on and the side. But when you're scouting, when you see a shark, see it, back off, back away, and then note where it is, come get us and then as soon as we're done with the one that we're at, we'll go catch that one, and we'll work it that way.

He had some real concerns about making sure they got better shots than just fish sitting on the bottom.

The footage that we wanna get is … gonna be difficult to get anything but a shark sitting on the sand and leaving the sand. So, we're gonna try some stuff where we scare the shark towards the camera. So what that will be is, I'll go and I'll position myself like in front of the shark, probably directly off of its nose or somewhat off of its nose, and then I'll call to you with an hour. An hour will represent what hour, from my perspective, you wanna approach the shark from. So approach it from, it'll probably be from behind at, you know, 9, 10 o'clock or something, and that's gonna be my best guess, because if you scare that shark out of the sand, then it will come towards me and you won't end up in the shot.

Once they had planned the dives and the filming, the footage revealed what is a rather long and complicated discussion about how they were going to access the wreck once they got out there. The captain of the boat, Dave Wilkerson, wanted them to "hot drop" onto the wreck. What this means is that he would take the divers up current from the wreck and drop them in the water, and as they descended the current would sweep them towards the wreck. If Wilkerson did his calculations correctly then they should end up right on the *Queen of Nassau*. I've done a few hot drops in my time, and it's a very uncertain way of getting where you want to be. On several occasions, I've been blown right past large wrecks (several hundred feet long) in the St. Lawrence River – and never seen so much as a shadow. In the footage, Stewart and Sotis were clearly not happy about this. Stewart explained that carrying a huge camera was going to make manoeuvring in current difficult. They were also both worried about finding the wreck if the visibility was poor. They both wanted a line hooked on to the wreck that they could easily follow down carrying all their gear. In his deposition Wilkerson stated, "I was under the impression, as well as Dan, that we were going to do the hot drop, which we've talked about previously, and I didn't know that was a prerogative of theirs to use a grappling hook, you know, until that day, and that's why I did not have it on the boat to begin with."

Eventually Sotis and Stewart won the day and Wilkerson not only had a hook brought to the boat but also brought on a mate to work with him – Bobby Steele. Fully equipped, they headed for the *Queen of Nassau*. It turned out that getting a line down to the wreck wasn't easy. Bobby Steele recounted what happened:

> The captain is using the GPS and the bottom finder to try to locate the ship wreck. I'm on the bow with the grappling hook and the line. Essentially it's like dropping the anchor, except instead of looking for a sandy spot, I'm actually looking for something to hook into. So, the captain set the boat to kind of drift over the wreck. He told me when to drop the hook then to try to snag it into the wreck. Once I was on it, I let out the scopes, let go of the anchor and I tied it off to the cleat on the starboard bow.

Wilkerson told the divers that they were hooked into the wreck and they could make their first dive.

Just prior to getting into the water, Stewart turned to the camera and did what's called a stand-up, a performance to camera in which he told the "audience":

> So, we're going down to 230, 250 feet using rebreathers, which gives us a lot more time down at depth and the exact amount of gases that we want. This is a new, well, not a new technology but a higher evolution of diving technology that lets you be silent underwater because fish are afraid of bubbles. And if you're a shark, you've got senses all over your body that are attuned to feeling movement in the water. And every time you breathe out on traditional scuba, each scuba bubble expands as it goes up, breaking into millions of tiny bubbles which sends vibrations through the

water and let's everything in the area knows you're there. So if you wanna sneak up on fish, if you want to stay down longer, be safer with exactly the right amount of gas mix you want, a rebreather is what you want to use. So we're here with Peter Sotis, Dr. Voodoo Gas ... Claudia, Brock. And we're taking the best rebreather in the world, the rEVO, down to film sawfish for the first time.

Aside from describing to the audience what they're trying to accomplish, Stewart was also promoting the rebreather company. In later court filings it was revealed that rEvo gave Stewart and Cahill special deals on their gear in return for promotion. Once again, thanks to the medical examiner's video, we can partially see what happened on the first two dives. Though both Stewart and Brock Cahill were carrying cameras, they didn't shoot much underwater footage, but they shot enough to give the viewer a sense of what the conditions were like. The water seemed to be stirred up and there was a lot of sediment. The divers were only able to see about 10 or 15 feet in any direction. In fact the divers didn't even find the wreck on the first dive. It turned out that the hook that the crew used was sunk into the sand, not the wreck. After the dive Sotis explained, "I took a spin on the scooter, I went around. Pretty low. And I was afraid of losing them. I was trying to keep an eye on [Claudia's] light, got them on the line, but a couple of times I lost her light and I miraculously found it again. It's like, whoa, this isn't going to work." Once they got back into the boat after that first disastrous dive, most of the interval between dive one and two was spent once again trying to put a hook in the wreck. Eventually Wilkerson was pretty sure that this time he'd found it.

But something else very interesting happened between that first and second dive on day one of the expedition. Stewart complained about experiencing tunnel vision. Later Cahill described it as "lightheadedness and, like you mentioned, a narrowing of his vision, ability to see, and feeling fatigued." But in the video, Stewart was much more definitive about what had happened. He told Peter and Claudia Sotis, "We were at the bottom in 215 feet or so, and by the time we got down there, I was working pretty hard and so I built up a bunch of carbon dioxide on my body and I started to get tunnel vision, almost like you're going to faint, where I get, you know, I was less aware of what was going on around me, which is really strange. And also, because the visibility is so poor, you can't really tell how far things are away or which direction, it's really disorienting." Claudia, a physician, responded by telling him, "If you're rebreathing CO_2, you get a CO_2 hit and that's usually a faulty machine. And most people say, oh, you get a CO_2 hit, it has to be the rebreather. Many times it's not the rebreather at all, it's that you're working so hard and you're generating so much CO_2 and you can't, you can't get rid of it, so it builds up, builds up, builds up, until you start slowing down and catch up with everything else. It's not the machine's fault, it's just you're overworking." And Peter added, "You're still learning how to breathe off a bag, it's not just like breathing off a regulator where it's in and out. So, until you get more efficient.... That's why I don't like hot dropping people who don't have a lot of experience." It's an ominous conversation. Stewart was struggling to breathe properly on his rebreather. Yet he had tasked himself to hold a massive camera and try to film at the same time. The result was that he was overworking the rebreather and getting tunnel vision from carbon dioxide buildup. It's prophetic when you think that within 24 hours Stewart would experience some kind of event that would cause him to black out and drown.

After the group had waited on the surface for 40 minutes, they geared up for the second dive. Sotis again took the lead and decided he had a plan on how to find the wreck. He told them:

> At this point, what we're gonna do, we'll go down.... I'm gonna tie off a reel to the line and I'm going to be in the search pattern and when I can put the reel onto the wreck, I'm gonna tie it off and I'll come back and get you, okay? But please don't scatter.... I know you guys will be at the other end of the line, I'll come get you and then maybe we'll move the hook over at the same time. And ... then we've got a place in the wreck and that'll be good for the rest of the next couple of days. We'll be good to go.

The plan seemed to work well because the underwater shots this time show the four divers swimming around the wreck of the *Queen of Nassau*. The visibility again was only a few feet at best. They made a circuit of the wreck and then headed to the surface. They were down a total of 81 minutes. When they surfaced, it was pretty clear that Stewart was disappointed, though the rest of the group seemed happy that at least they'd got a line on the wreck and would be able to search it more thoroughly the following day. But Stewart was clearly anxious about the visibility. The group discussed what might happen:

CAPTAIN: With that being said, if you find them, do you think you will get good footage?

ROB: Um … if we landed on top of one, I could get, I could get some footage of it in there, yeah. It's gonna look dark and weird.

BROCK: But that could be cool, mysterious. With the low-light camera, I was getting some kind of cool shit of you, with eerie light and coming off the scooters and stuff.

ROB: Yeah?

BROCK: Yeah.

ROB: Yeah, I mean, we'll get something if we—

BROCK: If we find them.

ROB: If we can find them.

PETER: Well, they'll never see us coming, that's for sure.

[Laughter]

They're clearly trying to make the best of a bad situation. Stewart had some serious misgivings about the whole expedition. They headed back to shore having made two unsuccessful dives. The following day they made two more unsuccessful dives. Again the visibility was poor and they found no sharks. At that point, they made a series of decisions that would ultimately add up to a fatal third dive.

CHAPTER 8

I haven't been lucky diving in the Florida Keys. Now, to be fair, I haven't spent a huge amount of time in the water. I've been to the Keys twice, and both times it's been to film underwater sequences for my documentary *The Third Dive*. Regrettably, on both occasions, while the weather was spectacular, warm and sunny, the water was rough. On my first trip the swells were so violent that virtually everyone on board was sick. Those swells created poor visibility underwater and that meant our filming was less than successful. But underwater filming can be like that. You can spend a lot of money in a very short period of time trying to get shots you need for your film, and arrive at your location to find perfect conditions. Then the weather changes, a current unexpectedly reverses direction, your equipment craps out or some other intangible phenomenon occurs, and filming is done. Even when all the various components line up to allow you to get in the water and film, it's often hard to get the shots you want: sea life isn't very co-operative. One wrong kick of a fin and suddenly you've stirred up the bottom and can't see a thing. Communication between the people underwater trying to film is very difficult: I've tried hand signals, writing on slates, I've even tried using full face masks that allow for direct talking between the director and camera person. Regardless, the whole venture can get derailed very quickly. The only thing I have learned is that you have to be extremely patient. If you think you're going to get the work done in a day or two, double that assumption at the very least. Maybe after four or five days you might have some success. Then again, you might not.

I wasn't surprised, given the complexity of the underwater shoot that Stewart was attempting, that after two days he'd not had much success. Given his earlier failure in the Bahamas to capture sawtooth sharks on film, he must have been frustrated when his *Queen of Nassau* shoot started to fall apart. According to Peter Sotis, the filming wasn't going well "because the visibility was so poor, which is common for that wreck. So, even if, I think even if we got face-to-face with a shark, I don't think it would have made it onto the video, I don't think the camera would have picked it up." Video shot the day before showed that the visibility was limited to about ten feet. Sotis said that using his scooter he scouted the wreck for any signs of the sharks and found nothing. Eventually, they realized they were not going to find what they were looking for, and at that point, according to Sotis, "when we got up from the end of the second dive [Stewart] and Brock made a decision to cancel diving the third day, there was no point in coming back. And they were concerned about budgets and spending money, and if they can't achieve something, there's no point in spending time doing something. The conditions weren't going to change and it was really impossible for us. Even if the sharks were there, we never would have seen them."

Once Stewart pulled the plug on the expedition, Sotis claimed someone had to retrieve the line and anchor they'd hooked into the wreck the previous day. "When we decided to call the dive the crew on board didn't have the equipment; they had the training and they had the qualifications but they didn't have the equipment or the ability to go down and untie the float ball from the wreck. And it was their equipment and they didn't want to leave it behind.... It was a pretty expensive float ball and line, and it was their product and honestly, it wasn't a problem to me ... so I volunteered to go down to pick it up." Like much about the death of Rob Stewart, there are multiple versions of what happened on that third dive.

In fact nobody can even agree on whether the dive was needed in the first place. The crew on the boat, deck hand Bobby Steele and Captain Dave Wilkerson, both said there was no reason to go down and retrieve the hook. In a legal deposition, Steele said, "Peter volunteered to go down and get it. At first Dave said, you know, you don't have to because Jeff and Dan from Horizon were planning on being here to go diving tomorrow anyway." Steele said that Sotis insisted on going, "and then Peter said – 'It's fine. I can go get it now.'" But when pressed by one of the lawyers at the deposition, Steele was vague about how hard the boat captain had pressed Sotis not to go, and there's much debate about whether anyone had plans to come out the following day to dive and retrieve the gear. In fact that theory didn't appear in any statements until months after the accident. Skipper Dave Wilkerson's written statement to the sheriff's office, made the night of the accident, simply said, "There was a mooring line secured to the wreck for ascent and descent. The third dive was to remove the line since the next dives were cancelled." Sotis' wife, Claudia, spoke with me and, perhaps not surprisingly, agreed with her husband's account: "Then the question was, what are we going to do about the float ball? And there was no way for the boat to retrieve it, they didn't offer any other means of dealing with it ... and then Peter volunteered to go down and get the ball." And when I asked her if the boat captain told Sotis not to bother because other divers were going to be on the site the following day, Claudia vehemently denied this: "Peter would have been happy to say, okay, fine, that's his ball.... If anything, he was doing the boat a favour, if they were going to come and take care of the ball themselves, there would have been no reason for Peter to go in."

Whether there was or wasn't a need to retrieve the anchor, Sotis geared up and prepared to go in. At that point, there's a second narrative that nobody can seem to agree on: whether Peter Sotis asked for someone to go with him. This is an important point because if Sotis asked Stewart to go, then it increases his liability in any court case. But Sotis said, "I'm really fast at getting myself together and getting in the water because I do this all the time, and I was already preparing to get in the water and Rob wanted to come." I can assert that in the two days of diving I did with Sotis, he was indeed very fast at gearing up. He sat around waiting for me on all four dives. On the day in question, Sotis claimed he tried to dissuade Stewart from coming. "I told him no a couple of times. I said, no, I'm fine; I'll just go down and pick it up, finish doing what you're doing. And he really pushed, he wanted to go, and the captain approved it and thought it was a better idea if there were two of us in the water anyway. So I said okay." Again, Claudia supported her husband's narrative: "Rob volunteered himself to go. And Peter said, no, it's okay, I'll just go get it, and Rob insisted on coming with Peter.... Peter would have just ... jumped in, gone down the line, pulled the float ball, come right back up, and Peter doesn't need any hand-holding or company or anything like that."

Skipper Dave Wilkerson also supported the narrative that Stewart volunteered. He did qualify that by saying Sotis made a joke about getting some help. Again, from Wilkerson's deposition:

Question: "Did Peter indicate that he wanted someone to go down with him?"

Answer: "Maybe like in a joking fashion, I mean, just not serious. Again, the whole thing leading up to this was, you know, like it wasn't a big deal, and you know, that's when Rob stepped in, he's like I'll, you know, I can dive with you, I'll go down and help you get it."

But Brock Cahill, Stewart's diving buddy, had a slightly different story to tell. When asked during his deposition whether Sotis requested help on the third dive, he claimed Sotis said, "I can go get it by myself, but it would be great if somebody would go with me." Bobby Steele's version is much the same: "He asked if anybody would want to join him. Rob agreed and said, 'Yes, I'll go.'"

Slightly different narratives, but they all had one common denominator: Stewart volunteered to do the third dive. Both men went by their own choosing, and they did so after an extremely short time between dives. When divers plan more than one dive in a day, they take what's called a surface interval. That's designed to allow some of the nitrogen gas that's built up in your body to dissipate. If you don't take that precaution, then you increase your chances of being affected by decompression sickness. The deeper you dive and the longer you stay down, the longer that surface interval should be. Earlier in the day, Stewart and Sotis had taken more than an hour and a half between their first and second dive – 100 minutes. Yet as they prepared for the third dive of the day, the two men had only been on the surface for around 25 minutes, and that following two deep dives to below 200 feet with a total bottom time of around 200 minutes. That was a serious length of time to be underwater and was certain to build up a huge nitrogen debt. Sotis maintains there was nothing wrong with what they did. He said the surface interval was adequate for the short dive they were about to conduct, and that doing a third deep dive was well within safety boundaries: "I've been with many people and we've dove three or more decompression dives in one day. So … the number of dives you do is not proportionate, does not increase the likelihood of an unsatisfactory event, in any way. There's no research to support that." There are a lot of experts who would dispute that statement, who would contend there is a lot of evidence to show that the number of dives you do in a day and the depth and length of those dives has a huge impact on subsequent dives you might do.

According to Bobby Steele, even the boat captain – no expert on diving – was concerned about how long Sotis and Stewart had been on the surface. Steele was asked by a lawyer, "Why did David Wilkerson ask Peter Sotis how much of a surface interval he needs?" Steele replied, "Because ... the surface intervals have been kind of long, like an hour-and-a-half or something like that. They had just gotten out of the water when all this discussion was happening." Despite the short surface interval, Sotis and Stewart hit the water. Steele said Sotis had a clear dive plan: "Peter explained to us that he was going to go down and untie the grappling hook, bring the hook up to a certain point to tie it off so it's not dragging on anything. They were going to use the line as kind of like their visual reference to make their ascent up. Once the line was free, we were going to be on station, staying close to the ball but not so close that – we don't want to risk running anybody over."

Sotis described the dive to me during our interview, from the moment the two men entered the water until they hit the surface again:

> We began our descent and we made it down to the wreck pretty easily, we just followed the line, and we had a plan. And the plan was that the float ball itself was tied off to a structure that was projected from the side of the wreck, I had tied it off to that, wrapped it around a few times so it stayed with the wreck. And Rob was to stay at that structure while I followed it down to the very bottom, which was 10 or 20 feet away, and grab the small grappling hook. And his job was to unwrap the line and create a small loop so when I came up, we could put the hook of the grappling hook through there so it would carry it versus dragging along the sand on the way up. So that's exactly what we did, we released it and then we began our ascent.

Sotis explained that the only anomaly on the dive was the wildlife they encountered. "We ran into a hammerhead shark that basically swam up to Rob and he could have taken a picture with him if he'd had a camera. So, on the way back up, we finally go to doing our deco, we were kind of laughing about, through sign language, about the one time he doesn't bring his camera we run into a shark. So that was about the only eventful event of that dive, it was just typical luck." Stewart's dive computer showed that the dive lasted 16 minutes. Of that time, the two men were on the bottom for less than three minutes. They spent about six or seven minutes decompressing at ten feet and then surfaced. There was no indication on the computer log that anything went wrong. Stewart's partial pressure remained at an almost textbook 1.2.

There is, however, one huge anomaly that the computer recorded – how quickly they surfaced from the bottom. The accepted practice for safe diving is 30 feet per minute. That doesn't include stops for decompression. In this case, the two men surfaced at a rate of 75 feet per minute – more than twice the accepted speed. That was most certainly a red flag. I asked Neal Pollock about the impact of that surfacing rate and he said that doing that many deep dives and surfacing that quickly put the two men outside the parameters of what scientists had tested. Sotis maintained there is nothing wrong with surfacing more quickly than the accepted norm, particularly from deep dives.

Sotis continued with his story:

> I cleared a little before Rob and he had another minute or two to go, and I wasn't hearing the boat and I wasn't sure if it was just because their engine was off or they were too far away or whatever it was. So I went to the top of the line, to the float ball, to see where they were and to let them know we were about to complete the dive. And they noticed us right away, they really weren't that far off, and they swung over to the float ball and Rob came to the surface as well.

There are several key points of this part of the narrative that everyone agrees on. Everyone agrees that they saw Rob Stewart give the diver's okay sign. When asked during his deposition, "When the divers surfaced, did you see Rob Stewart signal okay?" Cahill responded, "I did." When further questioned, "What form of signal did he give?" Cahill stated, "He gave his 'okay' sign." Cahill was asked a third time, "And was that his traditional sign, just the fingers – fourth finger touching the thumb?" And he responded, "Actually his was the middle finger. He always kind of used a different sign, but it was the same thing." Again the lawyer asked, "At that time – and I'm talking about now when Rob Stewart came to the surface – did he appear to be in distress?" And Cahill answered, "No, he didn't." Claudia Sotis agreed that Stewart showed no signs of distress:

> There was a little wave that kind of swooped over Rob's head and Rob was shaking his head and blinking [his] eyes, which means to me that he's aware of his surroundings, because I mean even though you have a mask on when you see something dripping in front of your mask, you blink, right, because your eyes say I don't want to have that water in my eyes, and he was shaking his head like he was shaking the water off. He was calm, there was no sign of distress whatsoever, and he was just flopping around and just being, you know, like he usually is, mister cool guy, but that's it.

Most also agreed that Rob Stewart did not have his "loop" in his mouth. The "loop" is the mouthpiece that the diver breathes through. Deck hand Bobby Steele, when asked, "Do you know if at that point in time Rob Stewart's loop was in or out of his mouth?" responded, "That's when I saw it was out of his mouth." Brock Cahill agreed that the loop was not in Rob's mouth and says it caused him a great deal of concern because "we were taught to keep the loop in our mouth until we were safely aboard the boat." Claudia Sotis agreed: "I saw Rob, his eyes were open, he had his mask off and his loop was out of his mouth and I said to myself that I need to talk to Rob about keeping the loop in his mouth after decompression dive." Skipper Dave Wilkerson was the lone dissenter.

Why should we care whether Stewart did or did not have his 'loop" in his mouth at the surface? Because the loop is connected to two inflatable bags called counter lungs. If you take the loop out of your mouth and don't seal it shut with a valve, water can gush into those bags, turning your rebreather into a massive dead weight that would drag you under. If, at the same time, you didn't fill your buoyancy device, or "wing," there would be no way to stop that from happening. Interestingly, in the video shot on the previous day Stewart did not inflate his wing at the end of his dives.

Once the two men had surfaced, the boat swung over to pick them up. Sotis said that by chance he was closer to the boat's ladder than Stewart so he climbed up.

I remember getting on the boat and sitting down, and from there, I don't remember much at all. I remember, I have a vague recollection of my wife and one of the crew from the boat talking to me. I remember them trying to help me out of my gear and I remember talking to them back. I was mumbling something about 10 feet or 10 minutes or something like that. I don't know what I was saying but it didn't make any sense. And eventually I came to and I felt like I was, I knew I'd had an event when I came to, I didn't know what it was but I also felt that it was only a few seconds. And it wasn't until days later that I found out it was actually several minutes."

Claudia said she thought something was wrong with Peter from the moment he got on board. He was having trouble taking off his gear. She said she went over to him and "I shook him a little bit, his eyes were open but he was not aware of his surroundings. So I knew that there was a problem, so I called the deck hand, I said, hey, we have a problem, I need some help here." Claudia, a trained physician, said helping her husband was a challenge.

His eyes were open and he was mumbling, he was resisting us getting him out of his gear but he would not follow commands. So I needed to do a physical exam on him at the time, he was in his dry suit and I can't check a pulse with the dry suit around the wrist and around his neck, so I said to the deck hand, we need to try and get him out of his dry suit.… It took a few minutes to get him all out of his gear, out of his dry suit, and we kept the oxygen on him and even that, he was trying to resist us with the mask.… Then he started to come around again and when he finally did, he had a full recovery. I mean, I did a full neurologic exam once he came back and he had all his reflexes, motor, sensory, everything was completely intact.

Bobby Steele, who helped Claudia, corroborated most of that version of events. He picked up the narrative with Peter in the water, stating:

Peter grabbed on to the tag line. He started pulling himself forward. The tag line got wrapped around one of those bailout tanks on the side. So, when he was pulling himself forward, it pulled the ball away from Rob. Peter, you know, he's got his fins off already and he starts climbing back on board. I'm at the back now. I undo the tag line from where it got tangled, and I threw it back out to Rob. Then this is at the point in time when I noticed something wasn't right with Peter. He started to act abnormally. Every other dive that he had done with us so far, he got back on board the boat, had his fins around his wrist, took them off, put them under his seat, unclicked both bail-out bottles and put them under his seat and sat down in the seat and got out of his stuff. This time he slumped in the corner like he was out of energy. That's when I realized something wasn't right.

Steele continued, "Somebody – I don't know who – said get the O2. I got the oxygen kit. I bring it back to Peter. Claudia had already got him out of his gear, and he was now sitting on the floor of the boat. I opened up the O2 kit. I got it all set up. I turned it on. I started holding the mask, the O2 mask, up to Peter's face then."

A diving accident is not dissimilar to a car accident in one respect – if you've ever experienced one you'll remember that everything seems to be both moving in slow motion and yet very quickly at the same time. It's usually over in seconds, but in hindsight there seemed to be all the time in the world. I remember diving with a young inexperienced diver in Lake Ontario on the wreck of the *Katie Eccles*. We were at about 30 metres depth and the water was very cold, no more than around 2 or 3 degrees Celsius. We'd only been under a matter of minutes when suddenly the young man was pulling on my fins and giving me an out of air sign – slicing his hand across his throat to indicate he had no gas to breathe. I handed him my spare regulator and he spit it out and tried to bolt to the surface. I knew if he went up too fast, he'd blow out his lungs, so I held on to his BCD and tried to hand him the spare regulator again. He spit it out again, kicked me off and bolted to the surface. I checked my computer afterwards and saw that this all took a matter of a few seconds, but at the time, when I think and wonder what I could have done differently, the whole scenario replays in slow motion, like I have a huge amount of time to think things over. In that case, after he disappeared to the surface, I slowly followed him up, fully expecting to see his body when I got there. Through some miracle, he was still alive. We got him on board and called the Coast Guard. After a short stay in the hospital he was okay.

I mention my dive incident because I think it's important to remember that the events that happened during Rob Stewart's accident all occurred in less than three minutes. According to his dive computer, that's how long Stewart spent on the surface from the end of the third dive until he disappeared, three minutes. And it was a turbulent three minutes. There was a diver down on the deck needing emergency first aid. The deck hand and Claudia Sotis were attempting to get control of that situation. Sotis was not co-operating, according to Steele: "He started yelling the words 'ten percent' over and over again. Then he got aggressive. His arms were kind of flailing around.... He's actually grabbing the skin of my hand to try to pull my hand away from him. I wasn't having it. I was going to keep that mask on his face. So, yes, that's what I was doing with Peter. Eventually he started to calm down and then come to where I could have a conversation with him later." Sotis said he has no idea what happened. "I've never had any type of a diving event on the water.... In all the years of all my diving, I've never had a decompression hit, I've never had an oxygen problem, I've never had any problem that you could – when you go down the list of normal 'what can happen to a diver,' I've never experienced any of those events, fortunately. Knock on wood."

Meanwhile, Rob Stewart was still in the water, and Dave Wilkerson claimed that while Sotis was being tended to, he tried to get the boat back over towards Stewart. "So I was back there, you know, on the stern yelling for Rob to grab the line, grab the line and that's when I knew something wasn't right. When he wasn't swimming for the line, which you should be. You know we're not moving that fast. He literally had to swim 10 feet to grab the line." During those three minutes there was a lot of frantic activity, easy to second-guess in hindsight, probably tricky and difficult to deal with at the time.

Interestingly, in the midst of this confusion, the only person not dealing with the emergency was Brock Cahill. Wilkerson claimed that while he was moving the boat towards Stewart, he asked Cahill to help. Wilkerson was asked, "Where was Brock Cahill at the time you told Brock not to take his eyes off of Rob?" He responded, "So there's the engine hatch that's on the center of Pisces. He was actually, I think, standing on the top of that.... I think that's the last place I remember Brock being when I told him to, you know, not take his eyes off of Rob." Wilkerson was asked again, "Where was he facing at the time that you told Brock Cahill not to take his eyes off Rob?" and responded, "He was facing off the stern where Rob was." Wilkerson is asked a third time, "And at any time before Rob disappeared from sight or you were told by Brock that Rob disappeared from sight, had Brock ever alerted you to any situation that his friend was in distress?" Wilkerson responded, "Not at all." The lawyer continued to probe. "So the first time Brock said anything about Rob that day after they came back up in the water was that Rob disappeared?" Wilkerson responded, "Where is Rob, and that's about the very quick period that it took me to turn the boat." Cahill denied that this interaction took place. When he was asked, "Do you recall Captain Wilkerson asking you to keep your eyes on Rob?" He replied, "No."

Claudia Sotis said that she just assumed that Cahill and the captain would deal with Stewart. She and the mate were busy with her husband, "and Brock ... was standing there.... He didn't attend Peter at all." Nonetheless, Cahill seemed to be the first one who spotted that Rob Stewart was no longer on the surface. During his deposition, he was asked, "I know this is a tough question, but what was your reaction when you looked back to see where Rob was and he was no longer on the surface?" Cahill responded, "I basically screamed, 'Where's Rob?' And it was one of panic."

Wilkerson remembered, "I turned the boat there and literally the ten seconds for me the turn the boat around is when he vanished." Steele said, "At some point when I was holding the mask to Peter, I heard somebody say – I don't know who – but I heard someone in the background say, where is Rob? That's the first time I heard something." Sotis slowly recovered and said his first thought was, where's Rob? "I came to, I became very aware, again, it was, it wasn't like I was foggy after that, and as soon as I came to, I was feeling quite fine, and that's when I heard that they were looking for Rob, they couldn't find Rob. And at first, it just seemed like well, that's silly because Rob's right there, you know, because they couldn't see him or they turned the boat the wrong way." Steele confirmed that Peter Sotis' first concern was for Rob Stewart. When asked, "Did Peter Sotis have any conversations with you after he came to?" He responded, "Yes. The first thing he asked me was, 'Where is Rob?'" Sotis said, "They were looking for him on the float ball, and so I assumed, at that point, that maybe Rob went down on the float ball, who knows, but the last thing that was on my mind was there could be anything wrong with Rob."

In an email, Cahill described his actions during the event (his punctuation):

> i jump up on engine hatch to get a better view, and scream where is rob? as i don't see any sign of him. david asks should i call the coast guard? i say yes! call the coast guard! and hurriedly strip down to my skivvies, grab my mask and fins from my gear station, jump in the water and swim in the direction i last saw him. i don't see him anywhere. i do some breath hold dives down a ways but still no sign. i don't know how long i swim and search. after one of the freedives i come up to the surface and just scream, noooo! wilkerson yells did you find him? no! i continue to swim until i know it is fruitless. then i swim back to the boat and climb up on the bow pulpit on top of pilot house to look from a higher vantage point.

No one else on board the *Pisces* corroborated any of these details aside from noting that Cahill jumped in the water to look around.

Claudia Sotis was less charitable about how Cahill handled the situation: "He was completely worthless. He was, he was flopping around, he shone his light on the ocean, he called his guide, he called his psychic to get a psychic involved and locate Rob." I asked Cahill about this odd phone call, and he confirmed that he talked with his psychic but claimed he had called his wife to tell her what was going on and she was in contact with the psychic. The psychic apparently said that Rob was alive and under the boat. By this point the Coast Guard had also been called. Cahill took credit for initiating this in his deposition and again in his emails, but Claudia remembered that the skipper handled the crisis. She said he was very calm: "The captain was the one, I have to say … I thought, conducted himself I think professionally. He was very calm, he seemed to know procedure, he called the coast guard. The way he talked to the coast guard was very on point, so it was the captain." The Coast Guard immediately sent out a boat to join the *Pisces*. Everyone was hoping for the long shot explanation, that Stewart might have just drifted away from the boat during all the activity and could still be floating around on the water somewhere. But it was a faint hope. The sea was relatively calm, the weather clear; it was unlikely that he would have drifted out of sight, given the sea conditions, in a matter of minutes. The grim truth at this point was – though no one was saying it – everyone seemed to know that Stewart had drowned. That was evident when I watched the video from the police body cameras shot the evening of the accident. When the deputy sheriff talked to Dan Dawson, the owner of the *Pisces*, he was told that the *Pisces* was marking GPS coordinates for an underwater search the following day. And when the police met the *Pisces* back at the dock to take statements, nobody was under any illusions about what had happened.

To this day, the accident that killed Rob Stewart haunts Peter Sotis. "I don't think there's anything I spent more time thinking about in the last year, what happened to Rob. I'd never had anyone.... I've never lost, I've never seen anyone get lost in the water, ever, and I've been diving for 27 years. So, of course I've given a lot of thought to it." And he claimed that despite the thought he's given to the situation, he still has no idea what really happened to them. "I've also been ... a standing witness and have been brought in on many conversations of fatalities over the years and it's pretty rare that we can define exactly what happened to a diver. We can come up with some causes and there's always the expert that was never there that can define it perfectly and he knows exactly what he's talking about, but unfortunately, with everything that I've learned so far, I can't find anything that matches up with what I know about diving that could have happened to Rob, and I do think ... that we'll never know." What was also unfortunate, in the next few weeks, was how some people reacted to Stewart's death. It changed this story from a diving accident to a complex conspiracy rife with what some have called evidence tampering and fake news.

CHAPTER 9

Within two hours of Stewart disappearing, the Monroe County Sheriff's Office dispatched two deputies to investigate: Nick Thaler and Matt O'Neill. Both of them were wearing body cameras. These cameras recorded significant stretches of the investigation in the early hours of the event. My research colleague, Jenny Cowley, submitted a freedom of information request to the sheriff's office for everything related to the investigation, and to our astonishment they turned over the body camera recordings. This video gave me an unprecedented window into what happened that first night – it made me privy to conversations that revealed a great deal of critical information. The time stamp on Thaler's camera began at 18:48. Stewart was last seen at 16:59. The first image seen on the camera was a grainy point of view shot of someone walking towards the United States Coast Guard station on Islamorada.

Within seconds I learned something that raised questions about the public narrative. In the days following the accident, the Coast Guard launched a massive search in the waters surrounding the Florida Keys. Captain Jeffrey Janszen, the commander of the Coast Guard in the Florida Keys, listed the extensive Coast Guard assets being used during a media conference: "As I speak, there is a Coast Guard C130 aircraft from Air Station Clearwater currently flying.... Coast Guard Watch Standards issued an urgent marine information broadcast, launched a station Islamorada 33 foot boat crew ... launched an air station Miami MH65 Dolphin helicopter with crew, diverted the crew of the Coast Guard Cutter Charles Sexton. So we had a lot of assets on scene, initially, when this started."

The scale of the search was, in Captain Janszen's words, "expansive, it was over 5,500 square miles searched.... This is basically the size of the state of Connecticut, if you imagine how large the search area is, and we have saturated the area." All very impressive and probably very expensive. But the critical question I've asked was, why did the Coast Guard do such a massive search in the first place? I asked that because the police video record showed that there was little doubt that locals, including the Coast Guard's initial investigator, believed that Stewart went straight to the bottom. Among the first words that Deputy Thaler heard when he arrived at the Islamorada Coast Guard station was that they were searching for contacts on the bottom of the sea and they'd found something already, "sonar pinging at 150 feet seeing a small object." Sonar is what the Navy uses to find objects like submarines underwater. If the Coast Guard was searching the bottom, by extension, they're not optimistic that Stewart was floating around lost at sea. That same Coast Guard member and the deputy go on to discuss the fact that the rebreather would give Stewart only 90 minutes of life support – that his two bailout tanks might extend that. Again, the obvious conclusion was that they believed he was on the bottom and had limited time or no time at all.

The next time the police body cameras showed some relevant footage was when that same deputy was down at the docks at Caloosa Cove waiting for the *Pisces* to arrive back. The first person the deputy encountered was Dan Dawson, the owner of the boat Stewart rented. Dawson acknowledged that he was in touch with the boat by cellphone, and he quickly brought Thaler up to speed on what had happened.

> Two divers in the water for this last dive. As we were helping him on board, his name's Peter, we were helping him on board the boat, getting all his tanks off of him, he was acting really weird and delirious, so we got him all sat down, the captain went to go get some O2, the mate turned around to get the other guy and he was not there anymore. When they both surfaced, they both gave the okay to the boat. We helped one on board the boat, went back and he was right there, hanging onto the line, gone.

Dawson had a few of the chronological facts wrong, but he was working with sporadic cellphone service and talking with his crew, who were still very much engaged in the crisis. Dawson seemed aware of what the sea conditions were like during the accident. There was little chance Stewart had drifted off. People on board the boat said it was a clear and calm day. There was virtually no current. Everyone agreed in their statements that they saw Stewart on the surface within a few feet of the boat. Then he was gone – everyone swore they only had eyes off of him for a matter of seconds. The boat captain said, "The time, which was probably 10 seconds for me to literally reposition the boat to get back over there to him is when he disappeared, at that point." Ten seconds, that was how long they lost sight of Stewart. That number changes in later statements and could have been as high as two or three minutes, but still, where could Stewart have gone in a matter of seconds that would put him completely out of sight of the boat on a calm clear day without any current? Dan Dawson tells the deputy, "Very low currents and then he was gone. I think he went right back down." Why was Dawson so sure of this? He's an expert with a rebreather, and he's probably well aware that when a rebreather floods – remember Stewart had the loop out of his mouth possibly allowing water in – it acts like a massive anchor dragging the diver down.

Back on the docks the night of the accident, Dawson tells the deputy that Captain Dave Wilkerson has "been doing search patterns and just marking things on the bottom so we can go back out tomorrow." The plan already, as far as Dawson is concerned, is to find the body and attempt a deep recovery the following day. In fact Dawson had already called in a local who had worked these kind of recoveries before. "Have you met Rob Bleser yet?" he asked the deputy sheriff. "No," was the reply. Dawson continued, "He's the captain of the Fire Department Dive Team in Key Largo. We've talked. So we're going to come back out tomorrow, another diver, we're gonna gear up and if we find something that we think might be it, try and at least recover." Deputy Thaler then asked Dawson about what Wilkerson has been finding and marking: "What's the things that he's seen? Are they on the bottom?"

"Yeah."

"Okay. And what's the depth there?"

"Two hundred and twenty. I was going to dive with the guys tomorrow, so I'm already prepared and ready to go."

Within hours of the incident, the Coast Guard was searching the bottom, and all plans being made by the Monroe County Sheriff's Office and Horizon Divers were aimed at trying to find the body on the bottom. So again, the question has to be asked, why the big search on the surface? There's also evidence that the Coast Guard had been told by at least one expert that Stewart was definitely on the bottom. David Concannon is an attorney in the United States. His area of specialty is diving accidents. He's litigated cases that have set legal precedents. He's also a diver himself and has worked with some of the world's leading dive experts. He claimed, "I was contacted by the Coast Guard … the day after Stewart went missing and asked for advice on what to do. And I told them to look right under the boat. I said he's right under the boat. They said, how do you know? And I said, well, in every one of these rebreather cases, the mouthpiece comes out, the loop, the unit floods and it acts like cement shoes, so we find them right under the boat, and that's where you're gonna find him." According to Concannon, the Coast Guard "said to me, well, the sheriff's got local fire out there, fire department, or the sheriff dive team, but I remember specifically them saying local fire department was out there at the site and we've got the surface. That was on day one."

So day one, and every piece of information the Coast Guard had, suggested that Stewart had drowned. Yet despite that, the following morning the United States Coast Guard launched a massive and very public surface search – looking for a live diver who had drifted away from the boat. Some suggested that it was a public relations gesture. Certainly the eyes of the world were on the Florida Keys. It was a massive international story. David Goodhue said his involvement in the story began when "I first became aware there was a diver missing after getting a call from someone in the sheriff's department. It was around five or six o'clock at night, January 31, 2017 … and then the next morning is when I found out it was Rob Stewart." Goodhue said initially he didn't know who Stewart was. That quickly changed. "I started to realize it was a big deal early the next day.… I began receiving calls from people in Canada, different news publications in Canada, then even the local dive community around here knew who he was, and pretty quickly, I realized this was more than a missing, a typical missing diver story."

The next few days would be a whirlwind of activity for Goodhue. He said he was filing updates online virtually non-stop. "We were continuously updating the site … during the three days he was missing, it was a constant update of the website, constantly fielding calls from outside, constantly calling the coast guard, calling the sheriff's department, calling the Navy." And Goodhue described the search as one of the biggest he'd ever seen in the Keys. He marvelled at the fact that celebrity friends of Stewart offered planes to come down and search the area. Captain Janszen, who was in charge of the search, agreed that "in my 30 years, it's one of the largest searches I've ever been involved with. Part of that reason was, we had a pretty good what we call datum, like last known position, we knew where Rob was. The weather was ideal for searching, I told the family that, Sandy and her husband, like you couldn't have asked for better search conditions on the surface."

Captain Janszen, along with the family, became the public face of the rescue effort, giving regular media briefings throughout. Brian and Sandy Stewart were extremely open about what they were going through, describing their involvement starting with the first call they'd received about the accident: "The coast guard phoned us about seven o'clock at night and said there'd been an incident. They'd been called in around five o'clock, they had lost Rob and they were doing a search, but it was a surface search, at that point it was, I think it was dark.... You know, our hearts just dropped. We flew down here as fast as we could and landed ... about five or six in the morning, as [the Coast Guard] were sending out the boats and the planes for the next day's search." The family was also not going to sit back and passively wait for the Coast Guard to do its job. They solicited help from the hundreds of friends and admirers who had stepped forward and offered resources. "We had 13 planes in the air at one time, to the point that the coast guard had to call us and say, can you call off the planes? There's too many in the air. They were worried about an accident, so they created a perimeter strategy where people would go into the core of where they were looking and then stay outside and check all the perimeter areas, and then would trade and rotate. And we probably had 40 boats in the water, and we had people walking the shore. I mean it was an extraordinary effort."

In fact, according to Captain Janszen, it was all a little too much effort: "We almost had, I want to say, too many aircraft and it was actually a safety concern maybe because when you stack aircraft in a search area, when it's saturated, it almost ... gets kind of unsafe, so at some point we just said, hey, thank you for volunteering but we really have enough aircraft." Janszen's second in command, the officer who ran the search, was Commander Clinton Prindle. He agreed that the search got a little crowded: "It's actually 10 times more difficult to coordinate air traffic than it is boat traffic. I mean you put 100 boats out there and as long as they don't crash into one another, that's okay. But we had, at one point, 17 aircraft, most of which were hired by the Stewarts, to search, and sometimes we had to work really hard to do traffic de-confliction so that the Coast Guard aircraft could get in the air."

A massive search, a huge amount of publicity: these were results that the family wanted, to raise attention about the incident and ensure that the maximum effort was being given to find their son. It worked. Goodhue said, "This story was one of the busiest stories that was, that we ever had on our website because of all the international coverage it received." Keeping the pressure on, the Stewarts asked for even more help appealing to the public:

> If you've got some free time on the weekend and you've got a Sea-Doo or a kayak or a canoe, please come and help and check. And I think the coverage we're looking for is from Marathon to Tavernier but there's other places. If you want information, if you can come out and volunteer, go to sharkwater.com, it's updating, that's Rob's own website that has, he's built and had it for years to support sharks. And if you can't physically come out to and you're not, and for all his fans and people that he knows out there that love him, they're worldwide right now, if you can't come help us, you can help by donating so we can keep hiring some people to continue to come out, and sharkwater.com will give you that information.

Captain Janszen said that he was even getting political pressure from Canada. He told me he got calls from the Department of Foreign Affairs asking questions about the search.

To the credit of the Stewart family, Janszen said they were extremely gracious about expressing their gratitude for all of the efforts being made. Brian Stewart told everyone, "On behalf of my wife Sandy and my son-in-law Roger, and my daughter Alex, who's been a rock in Toronto … I thank my family and I thank you guys." This press conference was given in the final stages of the search. Stewart had been missing for several days. The Stewarts, naturally, still held out hope and still kept asking for help: "I still believe he's out there. So if you can let your viewers know they can volunteer, please, please come out and help us." Captain Janszen described the Stewarts as touchingly grateful for the effort his team was making, even going to the extraordinary lengths of meeting one of his returning ships in order to thank the crew for all their hard work.

Regardless of all the international attention, the Coast Guard was only prepared to commit resources for a 48-hour search. They extended that deadline for the Stewarts, however, according to Commander Prindle: "We had gone up there ... to explain to them that in all likelihood, the following day, we would be suspending active search efforts and they begged and pleaded for one additional day, and so we gave that to them, Captain Janszen agreed to extend the search for an additional day, as a favour to, to the family." At the 72-hour mark of the search, Janszen stood at the microphone one last time.

> As I speak, there is a Coast Guard C130 aircraft from Air Station Clearwater currently flying. This aircraft will fly until sunset.... Once this search is complete, the search will be suspended. The decision to suspend the search is very difficult and it's not made lightly. Our hearts go out to Mr. Stewart's family, especially his parents, Brian and Sandy, whom I met with earlier today. I'd also like to thank all the agencies and volunteers who aided in this search for the past 72 hours. We had multiple air, surface and dive teams. I really do appreciate the coordination on this very extensive search.

Janszen seemed to genuinely regret that he had to make this decision, taking time to explain his reasons: "We also take into account survivability. In this case, a person in the water, a functional survivability is about 72–75 hours, we're at about that point right now." He ended by firmly stating, "We're confident that we've done everything we can, from the Coast Guard perspective, working with our federal, state and local agencies."

Virtually at the same moment that Captain Janszen made that statement, Stewart's body had been discovered. According to Goodhue, "When they found him, they had just wrapped up a press conference saying they were going to call off the search. This was late afternoon, Friday night, February 3rd. I actually filed my story for the newspaper the next day. And I was leaving town. I got a phone call from someone from the local fire department telling me that they had found the body. I turned around, went back to the office, we still had time to, to pull back the story.

I confirmed with the coast guard that they found the body." The body was found exactly where David Concannon said it would be – right underneath where Stewart had last been seen. Exactly where the owner of Horizon Dive Shop, Dan Dawson, suggested it would be. Even Stewart's long-time friend Paul Watson had no doubts: "We were in Miami, just dedicating our new vessel to John Paul DeJoria, and I got a call that he had gone missing ... down in the Keys. And I called the coast guard and asked, said can we do anything, um, and they advised us not to come there, there are too many boats ... but I thought that he would be found right exactly where he was because I knew how a rebreather could kill you. And he would have went straight to the bottom."

So why was the surface search done? Why did the Coast Guard create a sense of hope for Stewart's parents, for his thousands of supporters and the public in general? Why spend all that money – a figure that, despite repeated freedom of information requests that I've made, the Coast Guard have refused to give up – and deploy all of those resources when the Coast Guard knew pretty much where Stewart was within hours of him disappearing? According to Commander Prindle, "You always give the shadow of the doubt to the survivor, so ... it didn't sound good for Rob at the moment the call came in, based on the circumstances, but we were willing to run with a scenario where he somehow did stay on the surface." Captain Janszen agreed, explaining, "We get something we call a PIW, a person in the water, say on a lake or a beach or whatever, you have an eyewitness that says I saw that person surface, I saw him at the surface and then, and then they were gone. In other words, they were struggling, they came up and then they went down, I saw them go under but they didn't, they did not come up. You can make a reasonable assumption that that person drowned and is not coming back up, right. So in this case, they looked away...."

Nobody actually saw Rob Stewart sink, so according to Janszen that meant, "You have to assume that, we're assuming, from a search and rescue perspective, that he just drifted away and that was why you want to eliminate every possibility." An interesting point but somewhat disingenuous when from their statements amongst themselves, everyone, including the Coast Guard, knew exactly where Rob Stewart was from the moment he went missing. Even Janszen acknowledged that he was skeptical about the potential success of the search: "I said when it got to the point where I was talking to the family, I said, look, if it was me and I had ... resources and money, that's the first place I would look, if it was my son, would be at the bottom at the site." And that's exactly where another group of searchers, a less formal group of searchers, thought Stewart was. These searchers were about to create what might be the most intriguing twist in the story of Rob Stewart's death.

CHAPTER 10

The Overseas Highway runs 182 kilometres from Key West, through Big Pine Key to Marathon, Islamorada, Tavernier, Key Largo and ultimately to the mainland. There are some magnificent causeways that connect the islands – some of which seem to run endlessly, one of them stretching nearly eight kilometres. The road traverses some of the prettiest tropical landscape you'll ever see. But it pulses with traffic virtually 24 hours a day. During the day, if you get caught behind a slow driver, you can find yourself in a train of cars and trucks that stretches for kilometres, all moving at a snail's pace. The Overseas Highway is the jugular vein of the Florida Keys. Sever it, and all life stops. There was a bad accident on one of my trips and the highway was shut for several hours. It caused chaos along the whole chain of islands. Just after you leave Key Largo, heading southwest along that road, you may notice a tropical sea blue–coloured building on the right hand side of the road. The sign on the building says Quiescence Diving Services. The sign alone gave me pause for thought. What does the word mean? Just how do you pronounce it? Why would someone call a dive shop Quiescence? There was a small clue on the sign that asked, "Tired of diving in a crowd?" That's when I Googled the term. It meant "being at rest, quiet, still, inactive or motionless." It's a unique name for a dive shop, and I soon discovered that Quiescence's particular niche in the world of diving in the Keys was to create a more personal dive experience. Rather than cram dozens of divers on larger boats, owner Rob Bleser liked to keep the groups to a more intimate size. His idea must work, because according to his website, Bleser has been part of the diving community down here since 1977.

I wanted to talk to Rob Bleser. He was in charge of the search boat that found Rob Stewart's body. He claimed to lead a group of volunteer divers who had the skills to perform deep water body recoveries – a group, he stated, that was part of the Key Largo Volunteer Fire Department. He'd taken some heat in the media in the Keys about that claim. It seemed the local paper challenged whether he was actually working as a volunteer for the Key Largo Fire Department or was just out on the water searching without any real authority. I wasn't sure he'd want to talk given all that heat, but after a number of emails between myself, Bleser and his lawyer, and on the condition that his lawyer could attend, he finally agreed to an interview. When I met Bleser at his store, he was a striking figure. He looked a little bit like Ernest Hemingway, powerfully built, with a receding hairline and a lush grey and white beard. He had the kind of skin that told me he spent a lot of time in the sun – well tanned, leathery. He wanted to talk before the cameras rolled. He told me he was very concerned about one issue. He was offended that after years of being a volunteer fire captain in the Keys, the media was suggesting he was no firefighter. I thought it was an odd part of the larger controversy that surrounded Bleser and his team to fixate on.

You might think there wouldn't be controversy surrounding a group of people who spent three days out on the water helping to search for a missing diver. You'd be wrong. Bleser and his group have been at the centre of a huge amount of discussion. In fact I had to break it down into components to deal with all the multiple aspects of what many see as controversial. I started with that issue of whether he actually worked for the Key Largo Volunteer Fire Department. According to their lawyer, Jack Bridges, he didn't. In an email Bridges sent to a local investigator he stated, "Mr. Blesser is not an active combat member of KLVFD [Key Largo Volunteer Fire Department]. He may not vote in Fire Department elections nor may he collect reimbursements. He does not work shifts with KLVFD. In fact, he is not even a certified fire fighter." Bridges went on to say, "Active combat members are the only type of members provided for in our by-laws – none the less he represents himself as this and enlists a team of divers to help him." Seemed pretty clear. Bleser wasn't a member. It's not. That assertion by Bridges was contradicted by an email between Chief Don Bock of the KLVFD and the local medical examiner, Dr. Thomas Beaver, in which Bock states, "Rob Bleser is overseeing the recovery operation and is on the water with the crews." That statement certainly stated unequivocally that Bleser was on the water working on behalf of the fire department. Furthermore, when the controversy over who Bleser worked for surfaced as an issue in the local media, Bleser sought out Sergeant Mark Coleman of the Monroe County Sheriff's Office and had him swear an affidavit stating that during the Stewart search,

> I then contacted Rob Bleser, who at the time was Captain of the Key Largo Volunteer Fire Department's Water Emergency Team, and provided him with this information. We had worked together in several prior missing person cases, including the missing diver incidents.... Each difficult operation resulted in the successful recovery of the victims' bodies.... Captain Bleser advised me that he would alert the proper resources, notify the Fire Chief, and assist the U.S. Coast Guard with the search. Captain Bleser called back later that evening to inform me that he had approval and resources in place to conduct a search for the missing diver.

Again, the statement reinforced Bleser's assertion that he was out on the water in an official capacity. Yet, when I spoke with lawyer Jack Bridges on the phone, he maintained that Bleser represented nobody but himself as a dive store owner. Bleser, still smarting from this controversy, showed me badges and newspaper articles that detailed an extensive career as part of the volunteer fire department in the Keys and elsewhere in the United States. He seemed genuinely offended that anyone could deny his long involvement as a volunteer. I finally discovered through Bridges that the denial of Bleser's membership had been related to a lack of an insurance policy that covered diving activities. Frankly, I thought it was a bit mean-spirited to cut Bleser loose like that after years of service, so I had no problem assuring him that I would not portray him as a rogue non-member out on the water with no authority. With that assurance in place, he sat down and told me about the recovery of Rob Stewart.

Even before the Coast Guard was ramping up its search on the morning of February 1, 2017, Rob Bleser and Dan Dawson gathered together a group of people to start searching the bottom around where Stewart had last been seen. Dawson mentioned this to the deputy sheriff the night Stewart went missing. Bleser said, "I received a call from the sheriff's office, Mark Coleman specifically, who heads up the Monroe County Sheriff's Office dive team, and received the request to have our special response group respond to this missing diver." The local sheriff's office does have its own diving team, but, Bleser said, "We work together with the sheriff's office team ... depending on the structure of the incident. But in this particular instance, they only go to 130, the sport diving limit, and they're not allowed to do any overhead environment work, and our special response group is set up to do that. So that's how we ended up responding."

Once again, I don't have any issue with who asked Bleser to go out and search. There seemed to be lots of evidence to show that he was asked by the fire chief, the sheriff's office and possibly even the Coast Guard. It's a moot point. What wasn't moot was who he took with him. There's nothing "moot" about the crew he put together, and it was at the heart of the allegations of misconduct around the recovery of Stewart's body. Bleser decided to use the *Pisces* as his search boat – the same boat Stewart had chartered and been lost from. When I asked him why he took that boat and not one of his own, he talked in general terms about a size difference. But I couldn't see any difference between his dive boats and the *Pisces*. So I wasn't sure what motivated him to take the *Pisces*. Possibly it was because it enabled him to involve Horizon Divers – the shop that owned the boat – and several employees of Horizon. While Bleser and his crew searched for three days and the team on the boat varied from day to day, the core group, according to court documents, was stacked with people who had a potential conflict of interest in being out there in the first place: a self-interest in finding Stewart's body before anyone else. The owner of Horizon Divers, Dan Dawson, was on board, as were the skipper and mate from Stewart's charter, Dave Wilkerson and Bobby Steele. Jeffrey Knapp, one of Horizon's employees, was along for the search. That's four people, all of whom work for Horizon Divers, three of whom are potentially liable for Stewart going missing, all leading the search for the body recovery. By even the kindest of interpretations, that created a huge conflict of interest. It got more complicated.

There were two other people on board who had an even bigger potential conflict: a lawyer named Craig Jenni and his assistant Kell Levendorf. Jenni was listed the "chief investigator" for Witherspoon and Associates, the insurance company that held Horizon Divers' policy. Among his credentials are an expertise as a "forensic medical investigator." Levendorf works for Jenni's company, Dive & Marine Consultants International. Jenni was also a lawyer with a history of working on cases involving dive accidents and deaths. Jenni's role on board the *Pisces* was a little vague.

He's described by some people during their depositions as Horizon Divers' lawyer. Other people thought he was a lawyer for a dive certification agency, and one person was told he worked for the insurance company. Interestingly, any one of those roles would place him in a conflict of interest: all three groups were potentially liable for the death. Rob Bleser insisted he was just another volunteer. Yet the question had to be asked, when Dan Dawson and Rob Bleser were organizing the recovery dive, why would they feel it necessary that someone who acted as Horizon's lawyer and a representative of the insurance company be on board the boat? Reporter David Goodhue spotted the anomaly and said,

> The only red flag out of that list of names, I would say is Jenni, the attorney and the investigator. The other ones, at the time ... maybe they would be the proper people to go out there because they were there when the body was lost. I mean ... like I said, it might be a little bit more of a red flag that the attorney was on board.... He's not only an attorney, he's also, he also does forensic investigations for these types of dive accidents and I would wonder why he felt it was important for him to be down there. Why, why it was so important to have Jenni on that, on that recovery team because that's what he does, and that would raise a flag, that he investigates forensics, he's a forensic investigator, usually for lawsuits involving dive accidents.

When medical examiner Dr. Thomas Beaver, who was ultimately responsible for any recovery and transportation of Stewart's body, found out who was going out to search, he immediately objected. He sent the fire chief an email clearly stating, "At this point I am uncomfortable, with the commercial dive company that was involved in the incident also being involved in the investigation (recovery of the body is a crucial part of that). I am aware of the technical nature of the dive and the personnel limitations. If we can not find alternative technical divers then we must carefully monitor all of the recovery efforts." Beaver later told me there were all kinds of reasons that he was uncomfortable with this arrangement. He didn't know the cause of death yet. It was possible that it might be tied to something that Horizon was responsible for. "We don't know what happened. We don't know, it might have been an error in the mixture of the gas that Horizon Divers mixed for Rob Stewart. It might be an error in the equipment that they, that he used.... We don't know why [he died] at the point where they're involved in this recovery." Beaver was clearly worried about a conflict of interest. He was immediately reassured by the fire chief, who told him that Rob Bleser would "be going out with Horizon Divers tomorrow and will be responsible for maintaining the integrity of the scene." But Beaver said that didn't reassure him. His bottom line was that he wanted to be on board the boat so that he could personally supervise any recovery. Under Florida law, he was the only one authorized to take possession of a body, "and I approached the Key Largo fire rescue people that were supposedly handling the underwater search and I asked them to be involved in the process, specifically, I contacted Rob Bleser." To his surprise, Beaver claimed,

> they wouldn't communicate with me. I would call people, they wouldn't take my call, they wouldn't return my call. I would send emails, there's an email trail, and people would send me, they would say, well, I'm not handling that, so and so is handling that. I would contact so and so and they would say, well, I'm not handling that, the other guy is handling that. And they would just send me on this runaround and basically, I was just chasing my tail. I couldn't find anybody who wanted to take charge of it. But I knew who was in charge and, and the person that was in charge wouldn't return my phone calls, wouldn't involved me in any way.

When I interviewed Bleser he claimed he didn't the get the messages Beaver had left him, "had no idea that he was interested in being there, he'd never been on one before. I had a relationship with the medical examiner here at our facility for some other things and he had my cellphone number, he never called me on my cellphone number." Yet when I pressed him on the matter, he finally acknowledged, "I think he called my business one time, left a message for me, but I had no idea that he might have an interest in going out.... We were on the water for three days ... putting equipment together, trying to make sure equipment functions, you know, trying to make sure the stuff works ... and had no idea that the medical examiner was at all interested in coming out there." It seemed unusual to me that if the medical examiner left a message at Bleser's store, his employees would not feel it was important to pass on that message, particularly if it had to do with the work Bleser was involved with out on the ocean at that time. And when I asked him about any emails he might have received, Bleser also acknowledged that he might have received an email, though he says he didn't check his mail until several days after the search was complete. "I didn't look at my emails while we were doing this, so I did see after the fact that he had fired off a question as to what was going on and he should be in the loop somehow, and he had fired it off to the fire chief and the fire chief had responded back to him, saying that I was on the scene and was used to handling evidence, evidentiary materials and that it would be handled accordingly and it'd be handled carefully. That's all I ever knew about it."

So ultimately, Bleser acknowledged a couple of points of contact between himself and Beaver during the search but still affirmed that he had no idea Beaver wanted to join him and his crew. Beaver said this was just not true. He pointed out that the Noah Cullen case had involved Bleser, who had organized that recovery dive. After that hadn't worked out, Beaver claimed he had a conversation with Bleser and told him that on future diver recoveries, he wanted to be there. I asked Bleser about this in an email and he didn't respond. I think it's reasonable to say that Bleser could have been aware that Beaver was trying to contact him about the Stewart recovery. The question then has to be asked, why didn't Bleser respond? What reason might Bleser have for not wanting the medical examiner on board? The whole scenario raised an enormous red flag for Beaver about what was really going on during that search and recovery: "Now we don't know what they did, we have only their word and they have a self interest, so we don't know, really, what they did. I have some ideas but I don't, I can't be sure."

The final member of the search crew on board the *Pisces* was Brock Cahill, Rob's friend and diving buddy. It was probably appropriate that someone representing the family was involved in the underwater search. Aside from that, what was notable about his presence, however, was a couple of conversations he had with Craig Jenni and Kell Levendorf. These conversations confirmed the fact that Jenni and Levendorf were representing themselves differently to various people they spoke with – another red flag. According to a report filed by the Monroe County Sheriff's Office, the men misrepresented themselves to Cahill: "Craig Jenni and Kell Levendorf told Brock during the recovery that they were just volunteers. It wasn't until after Rob was recovered that they told him they worked for the insurance company that covers Horizon Divers and any dive shop that has Padi insurance." In his deposition Cahill was asked who he believed the two men were. "**Lawyer:** And who did you understand Craig Jenni to be? **Cahill:** That he was a marine investigator in conjunction with IANTD (International Association of Nitrox and Technical Divers)."

So why would the two men not tell Cahill and the police who they really worked for? While there was evidence to suggest that Jenni had a relationship to the dive organization IANTD, that's probably not why he was on the boat looking for Stewart. The most obvious conclusion that can be drawn from the evidence was that he was there as Horizon's lawyer and as a representative of the insurance company that might face a lawsuit if the Stewarts sued for negligence. That put Craig Jenni and his partner in a conflict of interest. Whatever they touched during that recovery process had the possibility of having been tampered with. Regardless of whether they actually did anything untoward, the mere perception taints any evidence. I phoned and sent emails to ask Craig Jenni about this misrepresentation and never heard a word back. When I spoke with Rob Bleser about whether having Jenni on board was the right call, he said that regardless of Jenni's affiliations, "I would have still asked Craig to try to help. We were, we were behind the eight ball. The chances of finding this were just so remote. The important thing was that somebody was missing and potentially dead and possibly never to be found, and in my.... We were the only ones looking in the right location."

Certainly this combination of conflicted parties on board the *Pisces* caught the attention of some of the lawyers involved in the Stewarts' civil case for negligence. David Concannon, who represents the equipment manufacturers, suggested, "Horizon and its cohorts were *masquerading* as a dive team from the Key Largo Volunteer Fire Department ('KLVFD')". Concannon went on to write, "Horizon itself has admitted that its search for Stewart was undertaken at the direction of its legal counsel in anticipation of litigation (D.E. 27)." Beaver went further, suggesting,

> The people doing the recovery, they have a conflict of interest because they are, they are involved with Horizon Divers, financially, personally, so they have a vested interest in the recovery of this body because they were diving off of a Horizon Divers boat....

To have a lawyer for their insurance company be on the team that recovers the body seems to me like a conflict of interest. So I put that together. People are trying to exclude me from being involved in the recovery process and we've got people that have questionable motives involved. To me, that's a red flag.

Later, after the search was complete, Beaver's suspicions would be proven to be well founded.

Despite Beaver's objections, Rob Bleser and his crew set out to search for Stewart at 8:57 a.m. on February 1, 2017. Bleser said he felt that rather than join the rest of the Coast Guard search he was going to concentrate on the area where Rob Stewart was last seen, "because there's always that potential for a diver to just be missing on the surface. But once I was able to gather up enough information about the incident ... my opinion was to make use of our assets at the very location that he went down." Essentially, Bleser and his group were working on the assumption that Stewart was dead. Remember that the night before, Dan Dawson had told the deputy that he believed Stewart would have gone right to the bottom. So, given that the captain of the *Pisces* had the GPS coordinates of Stewart's last known location, these locals had a pretty good idea of where Stewart might be. Once they got out to the *Queen of Nassau*, they demonstrated again that they had local knowledge that would make their search successful. Before deploying any divers to search for a body, they took the time to figure out which way the currents were flowing. Bleser told me he "deployed the safety diver down to between 60 and 80 feet try to determine what the subsurface current would be doing, so that we could deploy our tech divers ... to give the best shot at trying to cover what the last known position was."

In fact they decided to be even more exact. The current at 60 feet was different from the current at the surface. So they decided to see what the current was like on the bottom. If Stewart's body was down there, the bottom current might be pushing him in a certain direction. Only after getting all this information did Bleser deploy his divers. "On the surface we had a southwest flow from the wind direction, because it [was] blowing northeast to southwest. Subsurface, we had a northeast flow ... so we made the decision, made the choice to deploy the divers to the southwest of where the last known location was. Upon their descent, they got to the bottom and they went west, northwest, riding with the current." The divers came up blank. The visibility was too poor to see any distance and their time on the bottom was limited by the depth. They knew they would have little chance of success finding a body with divers, so "it was decided that diving operations would cease. We decided to redeploy the following day, with an ROV [remote operated vehicle], that we could control, without a time limit, and be able to run patterns in an effort to try to investigate the bottom as best we could. With just 5 to 8 foot visibility, 10 foot visibility, it was difficult at best."

They turned up the following day with their mini-submarine. I managed to get copies of the video the ROV shot. You can see that most of February 2 seemed to be taken up with getting the hang of how to use the machine. They sent the ROV down ten times throughout the course of the day, but some dives lasted only a matter of minutes, and they spent a lot of time weaving up and down and crashing into the bottom. By the time February 3 rolled around, Bleser seemed to have gotten the hang of it and they started their search in earnest. Throughout the day they managed four runs across the bottom. The underwater footage was a little eerie. Through a wide-angle lens the ROV swept back and forth across the bleak muddy bottom like some tethered mechanical dog hunting for scent. The bottom looked a little like the surface of the moon – endless tracks of smooth, lifeless mud and sand. There were few fish to be seen, no coral reefs, only the mud that stirs up when the ROV comes close, threatening to take away what little visibility was available. Mostly you could just see a few feet of the bottom and an expanse of pale blue water receding into the distance. At about the 13-minute mark of what's described as the final dive of the day, a faint dark blot appears in the distance.

Rob Bleser described the event: "It was looking for a needle in a haystack, frankly, but somehow, someway, the next to the last run on the last day time-wise…. On the very next to the last run, we were able to run into the body." The ROV actually lost track of the dark shape for a minute. Then it backed up, carefully retracing its route, and moved cautiously forward again. Out of the gloom you can start to make out features – a pair of fins, a white air tank, a pair of arms, a diver lying on the bottom, hands raised above the body. The ROV made an ungainly descent and dropped down beside Rob Stewart, then it pushed ahead and bumped into the body, finally coming to a rest in a swirl of mud. At 5:17 p.m. Rob Bleser radioed the Monroe County Sheriff's Office and notified them about the discovery: "Captain 25 to Central. We have located the missing diver with the ROV and we've just deployed 3 technical divers to go down and make the recovery. Will advise." Bleser told me that at this point his main concern, given the drift of the currents, was not losing Stewart again. "My first action, because of the direction of the vessel drift and the direction that the body was in, was to let out more line on the ROV because we were dragging away. I was just trying to swing the ROV 360 degrees to spot what might be around, hover off the bottom, with that 5 to 8 foot visibility, it was difficult at best." As soon as Bleser managed to get the ROV settled beside the body, the divers went over the side and followed the ROV's tether line down to the body. All standard procedure. But at this point, Bleser and his team made a series of decisions that will have repercussions for years to come.

CHAPTER 11

What really happened when Bleser and his team found Rob Stewart's body is at the heart of any controversy surrounding Stewart's death. There are at least two possibilities. First, the search and recovery team followed the rules by the book and handed the body over to the Coast Guard in a timely fashion without any of the interested parties taking advantage of their presence on the boat to gather evidence for a potential negligence lawsuit. Second, some of the recovery team took advantage of the time before the Coast Guard arrived to gather or alter "forensic" evidence in anticipation of a potential lawsuit against Horizon Divers. If the latter was true then this group, as Dr. Thomas Beaver suggested, was guilty of tampering with evidence. Much of the information that emerged since Stewart died has supported the latter interpretation – though some of the specifics of the event remain unclear. This matter has not been clarified in any manner by the Coast Guard, who, despite the passage of more than three years, have not released their report. Additionally, a couple of the participants refused to be questioned. Despite those limitations, here's what I discovered.

According to Bleser, the discovery of the body triggered a frenzy of activity in the boat:

> The impact hit us when the ROV spotted him and met up with him. Once the ROV was there, it was tough, it was ... real tough. You know, you have a feeling of relief but you have his best friend starting to grieve right away, you have a lot of things going on all at the same time and yet you have to stay focused on, gotta get the divers deployed, gotta keep this ROV without moving, gotta make sure the line keeps getting fed out to the boat and doesn't pull away.... It's a very emotional, hyped up dynamic point of time.

Bleser said the light was fading, the boat was drifting and it was hard to keep the ROV on the body. He claimed there was a real chance they could lose Stewart again: "We had three different currents, we had wind direction that the boat was being affected by and we had 750 of line out, so in order to be able to stand even a remote chance of finding the body again ... it was a mandatory thing to get the divers in as quickly as possible, before we lost that." In his sworn deposition Dawson described the discovery: "We're all driving around, we're all kind of doing the thing, lifting the ROV back up and in onto the boat, doing our stuff, just, you know, sitting out there hoping, and Rob finally says, 'Everybody get their dive gear on. I got him.'" Brock Cahill said he was the one who confirmed it was Stewart's body: "I recollect that the ROV had found him, and Craig asked me, 'Does this look familiar?' and he showed me an image on-screen, and it was a part of Rob's rebreather, and I said, 'Yes,' and he said, 'Everybody get in their gear.'"

Bleser ordered the divers over the side just after 5:00 p.m. on February 3. Three men dived down to the body, which sat at around 215 feet deep. A fourth diver remained at 100 feet as a safety diver to help in an emergency and to deliver decompression gas to the divers going deeper. Craig Jenni, Jeff Knapp and Dan Dawson were the deep divers. There's not much disagreement that getting the divers overboard to mark the location of the body was the right decision to make, though they could have marked the spot with a GPS and waited for the proper authorities. But Bleser contended there was a risk of the body drifting away, so they chose to go down to it immediately. This was the first of a series of critical decisions made during the recovery effort that have been questioned. The medical examiner was not on board the *Pisces*. By Florida law, he's the only one with the authority to move a body or order a body to be moved. He gave no such order. Someone on the recovery team could have phoned Beaver and asked him if they could retrieve the body. He would have been able to give them instructions about what they needed to do to preserve the evidence and then allowed them to continue. They chose not to. Beaver says, "I would have also liked to be standing on the back of that boat when the ROV finds the body and then we discuss the plan for recovery.... If we needed more video to get a better idea for where the body was and the condition, we would do that and then we would say, okay, this is how we're going to recover this body, and we would work out a plan and I would discuss with them what they would do and what they wouldn't do." Regardless of what should have happened, the *Pisces* recovery team chose to go ahead.

The second questionable decision revolved around keeping a record of everything that happened during the recovery dive. It was a critical part of the process, according to Beaver. He believed they had no excuse for not keeping any record. Beaver believed that, in part, because both Dan Dawson, the owner of Horizon Divers, and Craig Jenni, the investigator for the insurance company, were experienced forensic divers. Dan Dawson had an ERDI certification in public safety diving. Craig Jenni ran a business based on being an expert in underwater forensics and was a frequent guest lecturer on the subject. Yet both of these very experienced forensic divers set off to recover a body without a camera to record the event. In court documents filed by David Concannon on behalf of his client, the manufacturer of the rebreather rEvo, he's incredulous about this fact, saying, "Jenni, the so-called expert in underwater forensic investigations, supposedly failed to bring a camera with an underwater housing, as did Dawson, a certified Underwater Crime Scene Investigator Instructor, despite having three days to acquire the necessary equipment to properly document Stewart's body and equipment upon recovery."

The third diver on the recovery was a man named Jeff Knapp – an employee of Horizon Divers. He shed some light on the camera situation in his deposition, acknowledging that Jenni had a camera, but neglected to put it in underwater housing, so it flooded and recorded nothing. This explanation was hard to believe. Camera housings flood occasionally, cameras break down from time to time, and sometimes operator error means no images are recorded. I've done a fair amount of underwater photography, yet I can't imagine how someone could just "forget" to put the camera in the underwater housing. Even the most charitable interpretation would have to see this action as careless behaviour for an expert in underwater forensic investigation. But the team had another opportunity to record the recovery. Rob Bleser was operating an ROV – the one that had found Stewart's body. It had a camera on board. He had been recording every dive up to this point. Yet Bleser chose to pull the ROV away from the body once the divers arrived and record virtually nothing of the recovery. According to Beaver this was highly unusual. Number one, I want to have the ROV there to document everything that happened, so I think the ROV should have been pulled back but it should have stayed focused on the working of the divers. There are a couple of reasons for that. One, just to document what they do and what goes on. Number two is if the divers get in trouble, they're not likely to but if they did, if they got in trouble, I would be able to see that from the ROV camera and put additional divers in the water to rescue them or help them. So there's no way for them to know what's happening down there, from the surface, without the ROV.

Essentially, by happenstance or intention, the team created conditions under which there was no documented evidence to show what occurred with the body shortly after the divers arrived. Given the combined expertise of all of the people on board the boat – Rob Bleser, the captain of the Key Largo Volunteer Fire Department diver recovery team with decades of experience under his belt; Dan Dawson, a man who teaches forensic diving; and Craig Jenni, a man who partly makes his living as an investigator for dive accidents – this seemed to defy logic. This did not seem like a group of experts who were going to become confused or panic and not carry out a basic body recovery properly. The bottom line is that when the divers made their way down to the body, once the ROV pulled away, there is no record of what happened. Dawson described the dive: "We go down. It was getting dark so I had – we had use our lights. I was the first one on top of the, you know, going down the umbilical cord. We don't want to hold onto it and pull it off. So we get down to the body. I'm on the left side on, down on his left side."

Prior to Bleser moving the ROV away, you can actually see the divers arriving. Minutes before they swim into camera frame you can see lights playing back and forth on Stewart's equipment. Next you can see the body start to move around quite a bit. Just as the ROV is pulling away, it's possible to make out three divers clustered around the body. One of them seems to be working on something behind Stewart's back that requires his arm to make a twisting motion. This is the third questionable decision that's made – touching the body, touching Stewart's equipment. Again, Beaver condemned the forensic work: "So, the first thing they do is roll the body over to expose some part of the body that they don't need to expose and then you see this turning motion by one of the divers on open circuit that he's doing something to the equipment on Rob Stewart's body – unnecessarily, in my view. So it makes me suspicious, it makes me suspicious that they're tampering with the body in some way. And I would have liked to have been able to be there to ask them, you know, what did you do."

Allegations have been made in court that the divers did tamper with Stewart's equipment by releasing some or all of the gas that was left in Stewart's tanks. Lawyers for rEvo claim that was done in an attempt to obfuscate any testing that might happen on the gas mixture. That would muddy the trail and possibly exonerate Horizon Divers from any accusation that they'd made errors in the gas blending, errors that might have led to a fatal outcome for Stewart. Remember, at this point nobody knew what killed Rob Stewart. It was quite possible that it was a bad gas mix – an accidental contamination of the gas by carbon monoxide, the wrong blend that led to hypoxia. So getting rid of the gas would have been a good tactical move to head off a potential negligence lawsuit. Dan Dawson and Jeff Knapp both deny that they bled off any gas from Stewart's tanks, but Knapp also admitted that he couldn't see what the other divers were doing. Knapp was questioned during his deposition: "You guys then inflate the lift bags. You recall filling one with your bail-out, and you do not recall how the other one was filled, correct?" His reply: "Yes. I don't remember." A little confusing, but essentially he is admitting that he cannot say for sure whether one of the lift bags was inflated using Rob's gas.

Lawyer David Concannon took his allegations further. In his submission in court he stated, "The divers tampered with evidence by using Stewart's breathing gas in an attempt to inflate his scuba gear." And Concannon had some support for his statement. During the investigation done by the Monroe County Sheriff's Office a deputy writes, "I learned that one USCG member saw Craig Jenni inflate Rob's lift bag with air from Rob's tanks. When confronted about this, Mr. Jenni told the crewmember it was a precaution in case Rob went overboard." Stewart's body was on the floor of a boat that's 30 feet long and nearly 13 feet wide. There were solid railings on either side that were a couple of feet high. Jenni was telling the Coast Guard he's concerned the body, still in its heavy gear, would roll or slide 10 or 20 feet to the back of the boat, or up and over the railings, without anybody noticing, and fall off. That was his explanation for using Stewart's gas to inflate his lift bag. It seemed unlikely, and note that when the Navy finally did test those lift bags, they found trace samples of gas that exactly matched the blend in Stewart's tanks, and both of his bailout tanks were empty.

Back on the bottom, during the recovery effort, the divers made a fourth questionable decision. Remember, they had no authority to move the body. Granted, it's important that they don't lose the body, but they could have ensured that by tying off a line to the body and sending a lift bag to the surface. That would mark the body position and allow the team on the *Pisces* to wait for the Coast Guard and the medical examiner. Instead they decided to raise the body. Yet Jenni and Dawson are experienced forensic divers, so they should have been aware of how critically important it was to not disturb evidence. In his deposition Dawson described the procedure: "Craig takes my 140-pound lift bag, attaches it right next to the 50-pound lift bag, and Jeff proceeds to inflate that until Rob starts lifting off and going to surface." When the body arrived at the surface, a crewman from the *Pisces* jumped into the water and swam over to get a hand on it before it sank again, according to Bleser. "Once that body was on the surface, like you could physically see it. Go, go, go, get that over here now. We didn't want to go through it again."

Once Stewart's body was next to the boat the men hauled it on board. What should have happened then was that the Coast Guard should have been notified immediately. They should have been on scene and taken possession of the body right away to ensure there was no break in the chain of evidence. That was what happened, according to Rob Bleser:

> Us discovering the body with the ROV, the deployment of the divers to the bottom was a total of 29 minutes. That gave the Coast Guard enough time to get on scene. They were not on scene, they were within visual range, running at us when the body hit the surface with the lift bags. Once the body was on the surface with the lift bags, I immediately deployed a surface diver to get a hold of the body. Because it was on lift bags, you never know what's going to go on with the lift bag, is the pillow going to roll, what's going to happen. We weren't going to go through this again, so let's get that body onto the boat.

A little later during our interview he clarified the timeline: "The body got onto the boat and the Coast Guard was there in three to five minutes, something to that effect." When I pressed to make sure I clearly understood that he was saying three to five minutes before the Coast Guard got on scene, he gave himself some leeway. "It's clear in my mind. If it was eight minutes, but it was nothing more than, you know, that – I was looking at the vessel approaching us on the surface." So, going with Bleser's final number, the Coast Guard arrived within eight minutes. Remember that number.

The Coast Guard also claimed they were there when the body hit the surface. Commander Clint Prindle sent me a timeline that he says was based on the logs the Coast Guard kept during the incident. He said their boat arrived one minute after the body arrived on the surface. He also claimed that Stewart's body was left in the water for 15 minutes until it could be transferred to the response boat. By 6:00 p.m., according to Prindle, they were on their way back to Islamorada to hand the body over to the medical examiner. The problem with the timeline presented by both Bleser and the Coast Guard is that some compelling facts don't support either version. For a start, Bleser and the Coast Guard can't agree on what happened. Bleser claimed the body surfaced and they got it on the boat right away and eight minutes later the Coast Guard arrived. The Coast Guard say they got there a minute after Stewart broke the surface, that they waited 15 minutes to put the body on their boat.

Neither of those versions tallied with the records of the Monroe County Sheriff's Office. I was given copies of the radio calls Bleser made to the sheriff's office throughout the recovery. These calls are automatically time and date stamped by the computer recording the calls. So they give an accurate record of the timeline. Bleser made the initial call saying they'd found the body at 5:17 p.m., stating, "Captain 25 to Central. We have located the missing diver with the ROV and we've just deployed 3 technical divers to go down and make the recovery. Will advise." He made another call at 5:30 to tell them that the body of the diver, Stewart, was now on board: "Diver's been recovered, diver is on board." Twenty-seven minutes later, at 5:57, he called the sheriff again and told him his recovery divers were back on the surface and the Coast Guard still hadn't arrived: "Captain 25 to Central. Divers are up on the surface. We're about a mile west of Islamorada Coast Guard small boat and we're going to be transferring the victim onto that boat as soon as we do some forensics."

Twenty-seven minutes after the body came on board, and yet the Coast Guard were still a mile away. I asked the Coast Guard for an explanation of that discrepancy and they could not come up with any. Instead they told me the information they gave me was based on "my recollection" and that I should request a copy of the radio logs to get a precise timeline. I've asked for any information related to the event, even with a freedom of information request, and I've been told I can't have it. And there was something else about that call. Just what was Bleser talking about when he said "as soon as we do some forensics"? Dr. Thomas Beaver was shocked when I played him this recording. He said, "I don't even know what forensics they're talking about because … I've never communicated with them about any kind of forensic examination. There was no one there authorized to do anything with that body." The statement was potentially the proverbial smoking gun. I repeatedly asked Rob Bleser to explain what he meant by his "forensics" radio transmission. I sent several emails to him and he refused to respond. I also asked Craig Jenni to clarify what had occurred on board the *Pisces*. He declined to respond.

So there was a 27-minute unaccounted-for gap in the timeline. What happened in that 27-minute interval? What "forensics" were gathered by the members of the recovery team? In Brock Cahill's deposition, when asked, "You were just confident that once Rob's body surfaced, no one tampered with that body, correct?" he replied, "Yes. No one tampered with equipment – True." When asked a second time, "Did anybody on board the *Pisces* do anything to alter or change anything about Rob's gear?" he said, "No. The only thing that I remember is that his dive knife popped out of the sheath on his leg, and Kell made sure it was replaced." But note the careful wording of the question. Cahill wasn't asked if anyone took samples, downloaded computer logs or bled off gas. He was asked if anyone did anything to alter or change the gear. All of the forensics that anyone needed to get a head start on a lawsuit could have been gathered without touching the body. But oddly, the lawyer doesn't follow up with any questions about "forensics" that could have been gathered that didn't involve touching the body. Beaver had a list of what they could have done without touching the body: "They had access to the computer, so they could download the computer, they could also change data on the computer. They had access to the gases, the air tanks, and if they let the gas off of the air tanks, which I believe they did, then there would be no gas to recover and there would be no way we could analyze it to make sure that the gas mixture was accurate. So there's a lot they could do." I emailed Cahill and asked him again about the forensic state-ment. He claimed he saw nothing, though he admitted that he was dis-traught and distracted much of the time. He also claimed to have heard a conversation between Rob Bleser and Craig Jenni (Cahill's spelling and punctuation): "i vaguely remember rob blesser saying to craig jenni once he was back on board the boat, is there anything you need for your in-vestigation? craig shook his head no, and said he ascertained the info whilst in the water."

Beaver's conclusion is that "there's a significant gap in the time and they have the body on the boat and they have diving experts there. Craig Jenni's an expert, Rob Bleser is an expert, there's probably others that were there that know diving very well and they know what to look for and they know how to assess the situation. So they had time to do that and that is probably what they were doing." Though Beaver offered no names to support his statement, he added, "I was told Craig Jenni made statements to people that later told me that he said that there was noth-ing wrong with the equipment. He stated to them that they had done their forensic analysis and there was nothing wrong with the equipment, there was nothing wrong with the gas."

There might have been something wrong, however, with Stewart's computer. When I managed to get copies of the dive logs from Rob Stewart's two computers, one of the dives was deleted. Stewart carried two computers, both made by a company called Shearwater: a com-puter on his arm called a Petrel and a kind of heads-up display computer called a NERD (near eye retinal display). His Petrel logged the dive on which Stewart drowned as dive number 44. It had no way of knowing that this was someone drowning; the computer merely logged the infor-mation as it would any other dive. Yet the corresponding dive on Rob's NERD is missing. It no longer exists, though the dives numbered on both sides of it still exist.

So what could possibly have motivated someone on the recovery team to go through these convoluted exercises? Well, with advance in-formation Horizon Divers and their insurance company could make preparations for any potential lawsuit. There was some evidence in the court record to suggest some evidence was gathered in anticipation of a lawsuit. In a document filed in court in which each side tells the other what they're not prepared to share – it's called a privilege log – Horizon's lawyers wanted a series of photographs taken between February 1 and February 3 (the dates the boat was searching for the body) excluded from being handed over to any other lawyers, claiming that "the photographs were taken in anticipation of litigation and are in the possession and control of Counsel." What was the problem with that? Maybe nothing. But it could also be part of what Rob Bleser was talking about when he told the sheriff they were gathering "forensics," taking photos of the body and equipment.

The real problem with all of the so-called "forensics" mentioned by Rob Bleser on the radio was that whatever was done may have obscured the truth. The public, the authorities and the family will never know for sure if valuable evidence was destroyed or tampered with. Maybe only a few souvenir pictures were taken as mementos. Regardless, even the suggestion that this evidence was touched makes all other evidence that stems from it the proverbial "fruit of the poisonous tree." That meant that any investigation based on the forensic evidence gathered by the medical examiner, the Navy and the Coast Guard had to be suspect. It may be okay, it may not be. In the legal system, "may" is a fatal factor. In court, a lawyer would argue that no reliable facts could be drawn from any evidence that has the word "maybe" attached to it. That means the primary evidence in the entire case is suspect. Beaver was furious over what happened, saying, "They basically could have done everything that I did do, eventually…. It's not appropriate for them to be any way involved in that and again, if I was there at the time or if I had a representative there, then whatever they did do would be documented." Within days of the recovery operation he wrote to the fire chief, the man who had assured him that everything would be done by the book, and told him:

> I am very disappointed in the recovery of Rob Stewart. There was NO communication and NO cooperation coming from your agency. I am told that Rob Bleser is a 'Fire Chief' and is employed or otherwise affiliated with Key Largo Fire Rescue. My calls to Rob Bleser were never returned. Florida Statute 406 vests ALL

authority to recover human remains with the Medical Examiner. It also prohibits moving and/or tampering with human remains without PRIOR approval from the Medical Examiner. There was no communication with my office and NO approval was requested or given. I consider your actions and the actions of those involved in the recovery a flagrant violation of Statute 406 and a complete disregard for the authority of the Medical Examiner.

To this day, Rob Bleser maintains he did nothing wrong. "All we did was our job. That's all we all did, was the job that we agreed to do.... I don't know about the captain or the mate because they were running their boat, but everybody involved with the water emergency team part of this was volunteering their hearts and their time to try do to something."

CHAPTER 12

My second meeting with Dr. Thomas Beaver came during my trip to the Keys for principal photography. I still thought he looked more like a California beach bum than a medical examiner, and he had an easygoing west coast surfer dude personality to match that image. It turned out Beaver has the lineage to justify that look. He grew up in Oxnard, California, a small city on the coast between Malibu and Santa Barbara, just west of Los Angeles. Like many Californians growing up on the coast, he developed a love of the water at an early age. He said one of his idols as a young boy was his diving instructor, a former Navy frogman who introduced Beaver to scuba diving. Beaver also said his diving instructor impressed on him a belief that he was capable of doing anything. That left such an impression on him that rather than become a marine biologist – his first choice after he graduated from high school in 1973 – he joined the Navy. Beaver liked to joke that the reason it took him seven years to finish his undergraduate degree was that he could never attend classes without being pulled out for Navy training or to be deployed overseas. He finally graduated in 1980 and – still serving in the Navy part-time – found his way to the island of Grenada, to St. George's University School of Medicine. His timing could not have been worse. He started classes in 1983, the same year the United States invaded the island. Over a beer he told a good story about the surreal experience of being "rescued" by the Marines.

Despite the interruption, Beaver graduated from medical school in 1986. After completing a specialty in pathology, he began what could be described as a distinguished, yet turbulent, career. He worked as a medical examiner in California, Colorado and Florida, and at one point worked as the head of pathology for a large Texas university. By 2014 he was working as the chief coroner in Alameda County in California. He told me it was a large department, in operation virtually around the clock, seven days a week. While working in Alameda, Beaver said he underwent a life-transforming experience that ultimately led him to quit his job and take another one in the Florida Keys. He had been called out to a crime scene, a crack house where someone had been murdered, shot to death. When he arrived, SWAT was outside. They told him the body was on the second floor. "It's their job to clear the building," he told me, so, believing the house to be empty, he went to examine the body. While looking for shell casings, he noticed that the door to the closet had a gap along the bottom. Thinking a shell casing might have rolled into the closet, he opened the door. A man stepped out and put a gun to his head. "His hand was shaking and he was very agitated," Beaver says. "He kept threatening to kill me." Beaver stayed calm and started talking to the man. Ultimately he convinced the guy that "there's only one way that the two of us are going to walk out of here upright and that's if you put down the gun." To his surprise the man put the gun down. The SWAT team, by this point lined up in the hallway, immediately tackled the gunman. Beaver was furious. How, he asked, had they not cleared the house properly? The sheriff found out about the botched operation, Beaver told me, and launched an inquiry. Heads rolled. "I knew from that point on, I would never be safe working there." A lot of officers blamed Beaver for the aftermath of that inquiry. Another incident followed shortly after in which Beaver again found himself at odds with the department. He decided he had to find another job. He quit and moved to Florida.

Unemployed, he started looking for work. Beaver said that not having a job when you're a trained pathologist isn't a big deal. "There are always jobs." It's one of the reasons he chose that specialty – because it was a portable profession. He got an interview for the position of medical examiner in Jacksonville, Florida, and got the job, but it didn't start for several months, so he went down to the Keys to bum around, do a little diving, relax a bit. He met the local state attorney, and she told him they were also looking for a medical examiner. She offered Beaver the job. Ultimately, Beaver says, "the money was better" and "they had an amazing facility for me to work in." So he took the job in July 2014. He'd been working there for nearly two years when Rob Stewart was reported missing.

Now, Beaver's time in the Keys was not without issues. When he first arrived, there was the Noah Cullen case that he'd told me about on my first trip to the Keys. He was the young man who'd been out on his sailboat and met with some kind of incident that caused his death. His boat and his body were eventually found in 300 feet of water. Beaver pushed very hard to have the body brought to the surface for an autopsy. He said he'd been opposed by authorities who claimed the family wanted the body left where it was. Beaver said he needed to determine a cause of death. What if it was murder, he asked? The whole incident resulted in a very public confrontation, Beaver said, between himself and the sheriff. The sheriff in Monroe County, Florida, is an elected position. He wields a tremendous amount of power – not the person you really want to lock horns with. Beaver said that once he made an enemy of the local sheriff, "the sheriff was basically looking for my demise. And he knew that my time would be up in 2017 and so he waited patiently, and then he made sure that the medical examiner's commission reviewing my reappointment, wouldn't reappoint me."

As Beaver tells the story, he had a second run-in with the sheriff's office over the death of some utility workers just prior to the Stewart accident. Three workers climbed one after another into a narrow trench they were working on and were overcome with fumes almost instantly. All three died. A firefighter involved in the incident was also overcome with fumes and passed out but was later revived. When Beaver arrived at the scene he was not happy that the dead men had been removed without him being there to supervise. Once again, his point was that critical forensic evidence is easily destroyed if a body is not moved properly. The result, he claimed, was another public confrontation between himself and the sheriff. Rob Stewart's accident turned out to be the final confrontation between the two men, according to Beaver. I've reached out by email several times to the sheriff and asked him to comment. I've heard nothing back.

Tom Beaver had been working in the Keys for nearly three years by the time the Rob Stewart case came along. He was well aware of the idiosyncrasies of the local people – a very clannish group, according to Beaver. He was used to having to push to get answers, but for the most part, he said, he had a solid relationship with the authorities on the island chain. On January 31, 2017, he remembered getting the call telling him there had been a diving accident: "I was in the office and my secretary told me that the Coast Guard had called to notify me of a missing diver. And I called the Coast Guard back and asked for the details and they told me that a diver had gone missing and it was Rob Stewart." That name meant nothing to Beaver "until they told me that he was a film-maker and that he was on a film shoot when the accident occurred. And so, then I knew who Rob Stewart was and at that point, it became very significant." Why significant? Because Beaver said he remembered what happened when Noah Cullen went missing. He said he had a rather ominous feeling about how that might get even more complicated when the missing diver was also a celebrity. Right away he asked to be in on any search or recovery operation. He said he was ignored. "I complained to anyone that would listen, that this was just outrageous."

As a result of being, in his words, ignored, Beaver's first involvement came when he was notified that the body had been found and the Coast Guard was bringing it back to their station on Islamorada. Beaver was there well ahead of the boat – you can actually see his shock of blonde hair bobbing around in the midst of a group of people in some phone video given to a local television station. "When I got there," he remembered, "the parents were there and they were distraught. I think we were all distraught." Beaver said he felt so badly for the parents sitting watching their son's body being transferred from the boat to a hearse that he decided to make them a promise. "I promised [Brian Stewart] that I would get to the bottom of [his son's death], that I would find out and I would get an answer for him." Beaver felt he had a good chance of being able to determine not just the cause of death but the underlying factors that led to the death. What he didn't realize, he said, was that he was working against some people who didn't want the whole truth to come out. "It turned out to be a very difficult time to get any kind of information from anybody and to get all the facts in one place was very difficult." Yet Beaver said this should not have been a tough case. "Diving deaths are usually fairly straightforward. If the person runs out of air in their tanks, if they get entangled in something, it's pretty easy for me to discover what went wrong." Not this time; "this case, trying to find out what went wrong was next to impossible."

The day after Stewart was recovered, Beaver began a meticulous examination of the body and associated evidence – Stewart's gear. In Beaver's own words,

The first thing to do is to open the body bag. When we do that, we find Rob Stewart there in all his diving gear, everything, his dry suit, all of his attachments, his flashlight, everything, everything that he went down with is still on him.... We photograph him and then we go through a systematic examination of the equipment. His rebreather unit is still on him, we look at the valves, we look at the gauges, we photograph those things, and then we start to remove the equipment, piece by piece, photographing it as we go. Once we get all of the equipment off of him, and the dry suit and the undergarments, then we do the autopsy itself.

Beaver's main focus was to determine the cause of death. He said that's both easy and difficult at the same time. It's easy because as in virtually every diving death, Stewart had drowned. What made it difficult was to determine the circumstances that led to the drowning. Did Stewart have a heart condition? Was he using drugs that might have had an impact? Could an aneurysm have killed him? Beaver had to eliminate every possibility: "During the internal examination, all the organs are systematically removed and dissected, biopsied. We gather fluids for toxicology. We gather blood, we gather urine, fluid from the eye, contents of the stomach, we'll gather the bile from the gallbladder, all those things are gathered up to use for toxicology, if we need to." What Beaver was looking for was a clue. "I'm looking for trauma.... I'm looking for natural disease, too. Did he have a cerebral aneurysm that just happened to rupture while he was diving? Did he have any kind of medical event.... [for] our purposes, is a diagnosis of exclusion. Once we exclude everything else, if we have the right circumstances, we can call it a drowning."

The first results offered little to Beaver. "There was no medical, there was no anatomical reason, there was no physical reason for him to, to be dead.... He was in fine health. He had a good muscle tone, very fit guy. Internally, all of his organs were fine and looked functional to me. So, there was no reason, medical reason, for him to be dead." If there was no physical reason Stewart drowned, the next major piece of evidence that had to be excluded, according to Beaver, was the equipment: "So after the autopsy, once we've excluded any medical events and we've examined the body thoroughly, we've sent the blood for toxicology, now we turn our attention to the gear. So now we're saying, okay, he didn't have a medical cause of death, so now let's start looking at external factors." Of course Beaver didn't have the expertise to analyze diving gear. But he did serve in the Navy for many years and he knew some people who did have that expertise,

> so we take all the gear off and we package it all up. The Coast Guard helps us. They acquire Peter Sotis' gear, [and] even though he has had opportunity to change the gas bottles and we don't have his gas bottles, we do have the computer and we do have the basic rebreather unit. So the Coast Guard seized that from him, brought it to me. And now I've got Rob Stewart's gear and I've got Brock's gear, so all three sets of gear are, are in my custody and with the Coast Guard, I drive them up to Panama City.

Beaver claimed he normally took any equipment that needed to be examined to Rob Bleser at Quiescence Diving. But this time,

> I needed to get independence and I felt that the evidence had been tampered with. I felt that there was, there was a concerted effort to obscure my investigation to try to confuse me and maybe even try to hide the real cause of death. So this gear needed to go someplace outside of the Keys and it needed to go someplace very independent and very good so that whatever we found was going to be indisputable, because nobody's going to dispute the Navy Experimental Diving Unit, they're the bottom line. They're the ones that tell everybody else how things work.

They're called NEDU for short – the Navy Experimental Diving Unit. They are a group that tests the cutting edge of diving technology and physiology for the Navy. Beaver was well aware of NEDU's work: "If there's anybody that's going to know anything about this or find out anything from this dive gear, it's going to be them." He decided to drive the gear up personally rather than wait for it to be shipped, because

> I want to get to the bottom of this quickly and I want to move this along, so I'm not going to ship the diving gear. I'm also not going to take the chance that I break a chain of custody. So if there turns out to be criminal charges in this case, I don't want to break the chain of custody. So I put it in my truck, all boxed up and

packaged up, sealed with evidence tape, and I drive it up, I drive straight through from Marathon, Florida, all the way straight up to Panama City, and I got there in the evening, I had the supervisor in charge of the experimental dive unit meet us, we logged the gear into his unit.

That's about an 11-hour drive – from Marathon in the Keys to Panama City in the Florida Panhandle. But Beaver was determined that this case should be done quickly and without any possible room to criticize the methodology. Once the gear was delivered, all Beaver could do was to wait. He couldn't issue his own report until he'd seen the Navy analysis on the gear. That took two months. Unfortunately, when the report arrived, it ultimately shed little light on the cause of death. It did shed a lot of light on what did *not* cause Stewart's death.

The NEDU report was listed as classified by the Department of Homeland Security. But in September 2017 I was anonymously sent a copy. It's a long and technically complicated document, but there were some significant findings – some of which allowed me to cut through a lot of the false rumour that floated around about how and why Stewart died. The bottom line was that Rob Stewart's equipment functioned perfectly. NEDU looked at his computers and downloaded all the data from his dives. That data showed that indeed the dives were deep and long but Stewart didn't breach his decompression obligations at any time. He was using an aggressive 90/90 GF (gradient factor) and his computer was set to calculate the dive based on a 10/20 helium mix, not the 10/50 he actually had in his tanks, but nonetheless NEDU did not see those factors as deciding elements in the cause of death, stating that "although the gas mixtures entered were inaccurate and the GF were liberal, the victim did not violate the decompression schedule provided on the Dive Computers." NEDU gave itself some wiggle room with that statement, because all they were saying was that Stewart didn't violate what the computer told him to do. Of course the computer can only work with the numbers that are programmed into it. If those numbers were excessive or inaccurate then what the computer told you would be wrong.

The other important piece of information from the dive logs was what was revealed about Stewart's PO_2 (partial pressure of oxygen.) You may remember from my rebreather course that it has to stay within certain parameters in order for there not to be either too much oxygen to breathe or too little. Stewart's computer showed that his PO_2 was well within the parameters of where it had to be at all times. That meant hypoxia (a lack of oxygen) and oxygen toxicity (too much oxygen) both looked improbable. The report did note that the gas in Stewart's diluent tank (the tank you use to dilute your oxygen levels) was hypoxic at the surface and that "it is not known if the victim attempted to breathe this hypoxic mixture at the surface after surfacing from any of the incident dives." The Navy tested the regulators that Stewart used and found that they were functioning properly. They tested his buoyancy compensator and it was okay. They took the rebreather apart and tested the oxygen sensors and all the other internal machinery and found they were also working just fine. They tested how long his scrubbers should have lasted and again found that despite doing three dives, his scrubbers would have been cleaning out the carbon monoxide without any problem.

There were a few anomalies. Both of Stewart's bailout cylinders were empty, though no one saw him use any of the gas himself. This seemed to be an improbable situation. How would the tanks empty? If a diver isn't using his bailout gas, the valves would remain shut, meaning the gas wouldn't just leak out. So if they didn't empty on their own, somebody emptied them. One of the lawyers involved in the civil suit used this as a basis to suggest that the recovery divers had emptied Stewart's bailout tanks to ensure that there was no evidence in them that could harm Horizon Divers. The recovery divers deny this.

Stewart's breathing loop was found in the open position. That confirmed the fact that if it dropped out of his mouth while he was on the surface his rebreather would have flooded and dragged him down to the bottom. But with so many questions raised about who touched what during Stewart's recovery, it's really impossible to say with 100 per cent certainty whether it was open when it dropped out of Stewart's mouth or was opened afterwards. All the Navy says about the death is that "the victim did not make any attempt at self rescue once submerged."

While the Navy was working on this report, Dr. Thomas Beaver's life took another turn for the dramatic. He was fired from his job as medical examiner – more specifically, he wasn't fired, but his contract was not renewed. In Florida the job of medical examiner is an independent contractor position that serves by appointment of the governor. That way, so the thinking goes, the examiner remains independent. In Beaver's case, when the community board was convened to review the appointment, they voted against another three years. Beaver said it all stemmed from his disagreements with the sheriff: "There were three cases brought up and two of them were dive related. One was the case of Noah Cullen, where a body was never recovered, um, and the other one was Rob Stewart." Beaver believed that after those cases and his insistence that things be done right, the sheriff bided his time: "The sheriff was looking for me to be leaving and, you know, he was, his whole interest was in getting me out. For three years, he planned to get my, to have, you know, he was waiting for my removal, he was waiting for me to be, to leave, so, for my time to be up. That's what he waited for." Beaver believed that the Stewart case was the final straw. He said he kept pushing the sheriff to open an investigation into evidence tampering and the sheriff refused. "He didn't want to ruffle the feathers of the locals, he didn't wanna, he wants to get re-elected, he wants the support of those people. And it's a very small community and it's a very parochial community, and it's a very closed community, so outsiders are, you know, tourists and treated as tourists, and locals band together in a sort of us vs. them."

Beaver insisted that the sheriff had convinced the other members of the board to vote against renewing him as the medical examiner. I sent an email to Sheriff Rick Ramsay and asked him if he would speak to me about Beaver's allegations. He did not bother to respond to the email. But *Miami Herald* reporter David Goodhue covered the events and said that Beaver brought the misfortune on himself: "Quite frankly, I think he rubbed people the wrong way. I mean I think he was very opinionated on things, he demanded things. I think he would demand things from other agencies that he had nothing to do with and it just didn't sit well with people." Goodhue said that Beaver laid the foundation for his own non-renewal and was skeptical that the sheriff would have been involved in a conspiracy to get rid of him. Even Beaver himself acknowledged that he was a stickler for details. In a laid-back place like the Florida Keys, it wasn't hard to start upsetting people in the community, according to Goodhue. In terms of the investigation Beaver wanted to initiate into evidence tampering, Goodhue contended that by this point in Beaver's tenure as the medical examiner, he'd just used up all his goodwill and some key people didn't want to hear anything from Beaver. "I mean I think a lot of it was they didn't trust his opinion on it. I don't think – I certainly don't think the sheriff's department was covering anything up for a dive captain up here.... I couldn't see them going to that extent to cover something up. It wouldn't be worth their time, it wouldn't be worth it for them."

In a bit of an ironic twist, what anyone who wanted Beaver out of the way didn't realize was that according to Florida law, Beaver still had to finish the cases that he'd started. He said, "They were definitely hoping that my departure would end whatever involvement I had in the case and that it would go out as undetermined or something like that, but no, they were surprised that I was having to finish that case." That meant he wasn't going anywhere when it came to the Rob Stewart case. "There was no way that I was going to let that investigation go. I wanted to take it to completion, I wanted to make sure we had the truth, that's what I want, I just want the truth." So once Beaver received the report, he started putting the finishing touches to his own report: "I'm ready to make a conclusion and I want to because I want to do this as expeditiously as possible because every day that goes by, the family is tormented by not knowing."

Once Beaver determined that the equipment was not the issue, that Stewart did not die because of a failure in his rebreather, "so, now we're down, we're left with, basically, the diving type incidents." There was one facet of evidence that Beaver believed gave him the proverbial ace in the hole in determining why Stewart drowned: Peter Sotis. Rob Stewart did identical dives to Peter Sotis on the day he died: "Both divers using essentially identical equipment, identical algorithms, identical gas mixtures. They both have the same dive profiles. They did the same dives to the same depths for the same time. They're as identical as you can get two people."

Beaver also knew that Sotis collapsed on the boat. So he concluded that whatever happened to Sotis, there was strong probability that it also happened to Stewart. He narrowed it down to two possibilities: "Could it be DCS [decompression sickness], that's a possibility, and the dive logs help us there. And in fact, the dive logs show that they did push their decompression, so DCS is still a possibility." But Beaver said he finally rejected that diagnosis: "What argues against DCS is the clinical presentation. Peter Sotis gets air, oxygen, they give him oxygen, he recovers quickly, there's no further treatment, no hyperbaric chamber, no recompression, and he has no further symptoms. That just doesn't sound like DCS to me, in my experience."

Rob Stewart was an internationally known environmentalist and filmmaker.

Peter Sotis was Stewart's diving partner on the day he died.

Dr. Thomas Beaver sounded alarms about how Stewart's recovery was handled.

Linda Kruszka was one of the few locals willing to speak candidly about the Stewart accident.

David Goodhue was one of the first reporters on the Stewart story.

Chris Harvey Clark being Interviewed

Chris Harvey Clark Emerges from a dive in his research area.

Peter Sotis was considered one of the leading rebreather experts in Florida.

The author emerging from a dive in Harvey Clark's experiment area

The rEvo Rebreather that Stewart used.

Author rebreather diving with Sotis.

Stewart spent time before his trip to Florida investigating shark finning in Capo Verde.

Rob Stewart in Capo Verde

Isla Marada Coast Guard Station was the center of the search for Stewart.

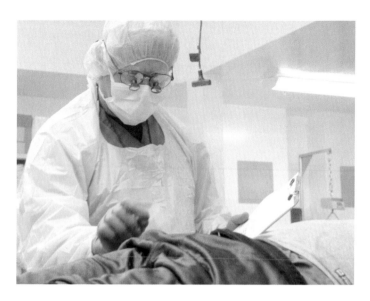

Dr. Thomas Beaver found no evidence of any physical problems when he autopsied Stewart.

The fact that Tom Beaver was an experienced diver helped him during his investigation.

Kruszka helped Beaver on the diving portion of his investigation.

Tom Beaver lost his job partly as a result of being a whistle blower on the Stewart case.

Linda diving at Looe Key

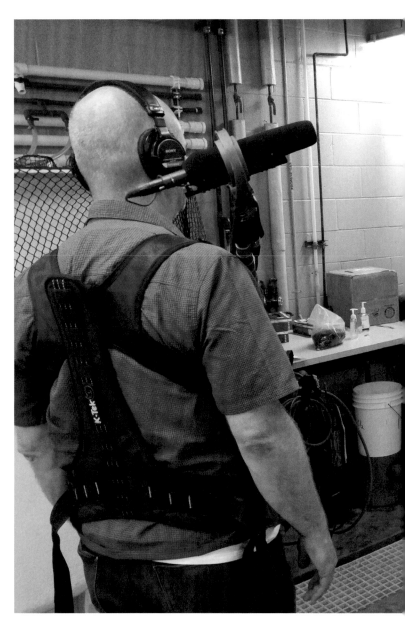

Documentary Crew filming Chris Harvey Clark
in his Lab at Dalhousie University

The only other alternative, Beaver decided, was hypoxia. Oxygen starvation would account for a temporary blackout that would cause Sotis to collapse and then recover once given oxygen. It could also have caused Stewart to black out in the water. "Hypoxia would respond like that. You get hypoxic, you pass out, they put oxygen on you, you take a few breaths, you come around, you're fine, so that's why I think it's hypoxia." It was a controversial conclusion, partly because one of the few ways it could have occurred was if there had been some kind of undetected malfunction with the equipment. Beaver was aware of this contradiction, but he believed the accident didn't fit neatly with any other diagnosis. He chose to go with his conclusions based on Sotis' symptoms. His final report stated:

> The witnessed events surrounding the collapse and recovery of
> Peter Sotis are characteristic of the clinical manifestations of acute
> hypoxia. Although the probability of Decompression Sickness
> (DCS) is suggested by some of the NEDU findings it can effectively
> be ruled out by the lack of any sequelae without recompression
> and further treatment. Decompression Sickness is progressive and
> possibly fatal without recompression and additional treatment.
> Oxygen treatment alone does nothing to address the underly-
> ing pathophysiology of DCS. Therefore, based on the information
> available to me at this time it is my opinion that both Peter Sotis
> and Robert Stewart suffered acute hypoxia at the surface. Once Mr.
> Stewart lost consciousness he lost control of the breathing loop
> and drowned. Therefore, it is my opinion that the cause of death
> is best certified as Drowning with the manner of death classified
> as Accident.

Beaver's conclusions are still being debated. Some lawyers involved in the Stewart negligence case dismiss his conclusion entirely, and they've got some legitimate basis for their argument. Deeper analysis of Stewart's computer showed that he was never breathing a hypoxic mix, so how could he black out from hypoxia? Experts in decompression sickness also contend that not every case of the bends has to be treated in a chamber – there are some soft tissue cases that clear up when the diver breathes oxygen to clear out the bubbles in his blood.

Once Beaver completed his report, he started looking for work elsewhere. Eventually he ended up teaching pathology at a university in Charleston, South Carolina. He says he's quite content now but for years felt he'd been treated badly:

> I was victimized by this third dive as well. I mean, it was one of the things that led to me losing the job, probably the major part of me losing that job, major part of me having to leave the Keys. It definitely destroyed my life. And I was very bitter at first, the first few months, I was extremely angry and I was thinking of what can I do, what can I do to express this bitterness. I was thinking of approaching the governor's office and some other options that I had. And I was certainly asking my attorney for anything, any ideas for that, any ideas for lawsuits and things like that.

Beaver says that he let his anger go after a year or so and has now settled comfortably in his new job in his new city. Despite the contradictory data, he stands by his analysis of the cause of death.

CHAPTER 13

The Coast Guard led the investigation into the Rob Stewart drowning. They got out of the gate quickly. You can see evidence of that in the video shot by the Monroe County sheriff's deputies on the night of the incident. A Coast Guard investigator was on the job within an hour. Benjamin Morris arrived at U.S. Coast Guard Station Islamorada just before 7:00 p.m. that night. His arrival was one of the first entries made in the police report: "Upon arrival to the Coast Guard station I met with the chief Marine Investigator Benjamin Morris who is handling the investigation of the missing diver...." According to that report, Morris is the one telling the police where to meet the boat that night. "Benjamin stated the vessel is out of Caloosa Cove Marina [and] would be returning to the dock after released from the scene." Morris led the group down to Caloosa Cove, at about 7:30, where the *Pisces*, carrying Stewart's film crew, had been based during the Stewart charter. Morris immediately met with the owner of Horizon Divers and the *Pisces*, Dan Dawson, who was also waiting for his boat to return to port. Dawson had already been in contact with the *Pisces* and gave Morris a general description of what his skipper was telling him. Morris met the boat as soon as it pulled into the dock at about ten minutes after nine. He worked with the deputy and took the initial statements. He made sure the crew was aware they had to go and get tested for drugs and alcohol in their blood – a standard procedure when an accident happens. All that is to show that the Coast Guard investigation got off to a solid start. The problem was, it seemed to ultimately bog down.

The result is that, for some inexplicable reason, more than three years after the Stewart accident occurred, the Coast Guard still haven't completed their report to release to the public. There have been a lot of theories as to why. I think part of the reason may be that the Coast Guard began their investigation based on certain assumptions. They ignored or downplayed key pieces of evidence. They came to a conclusion and then realized that the evidence they had downplayed might not completely support their conclusions. That's left them, I suspect, trying to retrofit the report. Stalling the release was one of the options. At least that's what one source told me, and it fits with much of the evidence I've gathered.

So what might they have ignored? I started by looking at the obvious. According to David Goodhue, many in the Keys assumed from the start that Stewart probably died because he was incompetent with his gear: "I would say there was a sense in the community, at the time, that maybe he was ... out of his league, in terms of the amount of time and experience he had with that type of equipment.... I think there was a definite feeling among a lot of the people in the dive community around here that he was pushing the limit of what he was capable of." An attendant part of that same theory, according to Goodhue, was that Stewart's dive buddy, Peter Sotis, was largely to blame for Stewart's death: "People were pointing the finger at his instructor, Peter Sotis. They were thinking maybe he pushed him too far, he maybe gave him an over-inflated sense of what he was capable of at the time, and basically that he was just pushing him beyond what he was trained to do at that time." What was not part of the initial theory was Horizon Divers' role: "There wasn't too much talk around here about Horizon Divers." Goodhue acknowledged that eventually people accepted that "there was a certain responsibility that someone on the dive boat should always have an eye on the person who's still in the water," but that was later in the process.

So did that initial omission influence the direction that the Coast Guard investigation took? Remember, the investigators lived in the Florida Keys. Many of the people involved in the incident, either directly or indirectly, were their neighbours or even their colleagues. And never forget that the Florida Keys is a very small community. A lot of tourists may visit, but if you look at the full-time population, it's not that big – only 73,000 people, 25,000 of whom live in Key West and 10,000 in Key Largo, leaving just 38,000 people spread out along a 125-mile-long chain of islands. A large part of the Keys is very "small town." Add to that the fact that there's a culture in the Keys of "one hand washing the other," according to Linda Kruszka. So the question had to be asked, did Coast Guard Investigator Benjamin Morris (and later investigators Chief Warrant Officer Dan Sammons and Lieutenant Brad Bergan) focus on

Sotis and Stewart as the cause of the accident to the exclusion of Horizon Divers? If they did, then that certainly would have skewed the results of their investigation. And if that was the case, did they ignore any other factors that might have been salient?

David Concannon believed that was the case. He claimed he was brought into the Stewart case at the very beginning and had ongoing contact with the Coast Guard as they worked on their report. When I spoke with him, he told me to keep in mind that "the investigators involved here are very confident in their work. I know that. I don't know that they should be, but I know that they are. They're highly confident in their work." Concannon's theory about why the Coast Guard was taking so long also revolved around the assumption that they had ignored key pieces of evidence. He believed that they only realized late in the game they'd focused too heavily on Sotis. Concannon said, "They ignored other areas and that would just be by design or through incompetence, frankly." His claim, he said, is based on having been exposed to the content of the report. He wouldn't elaborate on how but said, "My understanding of the report, which I have not seen and I don't have but I have had a summary provided to me, orally, is that they focus on Peter Sotis pretty heavily and they've always focused on Sotis very heavily, to exclusion of Horizon." Concannon felt the Coast Guard had not taken an objective approach to the whole investigative process. "I mean what they did not do in this investigation was take a broad look at all the evidence, objectively, and see where it leads. They took a narrow look at some of the evidence subjectively and followed it where that led but it's not the big picture."

There's still other information they don't seem to have taken into account – the possibility that evidence tampering occurred. Dr. Beaver had always been candid about his belief that the recovery team tampered with the evidence. Beaver said, "What they did I think does muddy the water some and it does make anything we do kind of…. It makes it less certain." I raised Dr. Beaver's concern with the Coast Guard on several occasions. I asked Lieutenant Commander Ryan Kelley, a public relations officer who handled most of my calls, how the Coast Guard could draw definitive conclusions based on evidence that the medical examiner believed had been tampered with. I never received a direct answer to that question. Kelley did say "they had taken those factors into account," but he could not or would not elaborate on what he meant by that comment.

Certainly there was no doubt that the Coast Guard was well aware of the possibility of evidence tampering early on in the case. Commander Clint Prindle was handling the day-to-day operations of the Stewart search. In an interview, he told me that the night Stewart's body was found he responded to an odd concern from Brian and Sandy Stewart: "I sent the Station Islamorada boat back out to the location so that we could take immediate custody of Rob's body and also of the dive gear because we knew that there was some suspicion that, that something had gone wrong with the dive gear and we didn't want anybody from the *Pisces* or anybody else manipulating anything that could be evidence later on." I asked Prindle what he meant by "some suspicion" and "manipulating anything." He asked for a "mulligan" and "restated" his next answer in an email, saying, "As for the suspicion of foul play, I didn't really have any reason to suspect anyone would manipulate the dive gear or Rob's remains. Brian and Sandra however were very concerned that one of the divers would manipulate some of the equipment; they had also alluded to a civil suit against either his dive partner or the PISCES crew." So Dr. Beaver wasn't the only one concerned about what was happening on aboard the *Pisces*. Stewart's parents were so concerned that they asked the Coast Guard to hustle out to the recovery boat and get their son's body and equipment as quickly as possible. So just how did the Coast Guard factor that information into their investigation? How do you factor in the potential for tampered evidence? I've asked those questions many times and never been given an answer.

In fact, at one point, I discovered another anomaly in the evidence chain and went back and asked the Coast Guard about that problem. I spoke earlier about a missing dive from Stewart's computer. I approached the Coast Guard and asked what that meant to them in terms of the accuracy of their evidence. I put it to them that if there was one missing piece of information then how confident could they be there might not be other missing or altered pieces? Once again they gave me a vague answer about "taking these things into account" but would not elaborate on how they might accomplish that. David Concannon has also pointed out to the Coast Guard that they've been ignoring information held on the dive computers. Everyone involved in the Stewart

166

civil case, as well as the Coast Guard, had access to Rob Stewart's computers, yet Concannon said the Coast Guard "never cared to look at the data that was downloaded from the rebreather until we forced them to. We literally, meaning rEvo, beat them up so badly that a lawyer in New Orleans, a lieutenant commander, in their legal department at their Center for Excellence, for investigations, said that you can't finalize this investigation without at least collecting this evidence and analyzing it." Concannon added that he "went up the chain of command, all the way up, and said this is gonna be, you're gonna make a mistake and we will have your head on a platter for doing it because we're going to get this evidence eventually and whatever you say or whatever conclusions you come to are going to be faulty."

While there's evidence that the Coast Guard were reluctant to incorporate certain information, that doesn't necessarily mean they are stalling on the release of the report. But there was one compelling piece of evidence that strongly supports the stalling theory: the timeline. The components of the Coast Guard investigation were not difficult to inventory. There's only so much information that must be taken into account: they would need a copy of the police investigation; a copy of the report done by NEDU (the Navy) on the gear; a copy of the medical examiner's report; and a copy of any information held by the Key Largo Volunteer Fire Department (the ROV footage and Rob Bleser's report). Finally, they would need to interview all of the people involved in the incident – there were five people on the boat when Stewart was lost. The Coast Guard would also have to review whatever rules, regulations and legal precedents applied to the case. But it should be safe to assume that experienced investigators would not be approaching this material from scratch so they would be familiar with much of it already. They might have to get a couple of additional pieces of information – Florida Fish and Wildlife had some involvement. They might want to get some meteorological information so they knew what the sea and weather conditions were like – but that data was all being tracked by the Coast Guard command centre during the search, so the information would have been easy to get. There would also be some kind of after-action report from the Coast Guard search and rescue team that the investigators would want to have in hand. Add those elements up and they are the principal components. Here's the curious part: all of those components were available within a few months of the accident occurring.

The Monroe Country Sheriff's Office made its last entry about the investigation on March 14, 2017. What sparse work done by the Key Largo Volunteer Fire Department was dated February 2, 2017. The Navy Experimental Diving Unit received the equipment on February 18, 2017, and completed their review of Stewart's equipment, Sotis' equipment and Brock Cahill's equipment by April 17, 2017. Dr. Thomas Beaver finished his report by August 2017. Witness statements were taken by the police the night of the incident. Brock Cahill was further interviewed at the Islamorada Coast Guard station on the night of February 3 when Stewart's body was recovered. Any further interviews could have been easily done during that same time period. So essentially, almost everything the Coast Guard needed for their investigation was in their hands by August 2017. I've spoken to some of the key subjects on the boat and they do mention that the Coast Guard interviewed them again within a few months of the incident. So if you really want to give the Coast Guard the benefit of the doubt, they should have been able to deliver their investigation by October 2017 at the latest. That's nearly three years and counting from the present day.

Not everyone believes in the theory that the Coast Guard were stalling the release of the report. Captain Jeff Janszen, the man in charge of the Coast Guard in the Florida Keys, has suggested it may be simple bureaucratic inefficiency. "I'm always embarrassed to say that but 30 years I've been in, I've never seen a serious marine casualty get resolved. And I don't know if it's legal review up there, I'm not a lawyer, but I don't know why these things take so long but that's just, that's just the reality." There was some support for that theory. A media liaison department that I was asked to use – the U.S. Coast Guard Motion Picture & Television Office – took weeks to respond to the most rudimentary question or request. For example, I asked them for an interview in April 2019 with the captain in command of the Coast Guard in the Florida Keys at the time of Stewart's accident. It took them four months and multiple email reminders about the interview before they finally were able to arrange it. An interview request to many media departments outside the Coast Guard can often be delivered within days if not hours.

I also put in a freedom of information request to the Coast Guard for data on the start dates and end dates of every death-related investigation they'd done for the past five years. It took them six months to send me a couple of columns of figures, but when it arrived, it showed that the average time for an investigation was 18 months, which the Stewart case exceeds by a considerable margin. But it also showed that there were 32 investigations that had stretched on for considerably longer – still unresolved after an average of more than 40 months. So maybe Captain Janszen was right: there may not be some conspiracy of silence, it may be simple bureaucratic inefficiency. Then again, Captain Janszen has an interest in the Coast Guard not looking incompetent in the Stewart incident.

David Concannon has another theory. His bottom line was that aside from the glaring mistakes the Coast Guard made throughout the process, they're also shy of litigation, and that may be a motivating factor in keeping the report under wraps: "I believe, a suspicious, a suspicion, a hunch, that the Coast Guard now has a policy of not releasing reports in cases that are going to result in litigation or have resulted in litigation.... They don't want to get involved in litigation. I think they're sitting on the report for that reason." And yet that doesn't explain everything. According to a spokesperson from the Coast Guard, U.S. law prohibits the use of their reports as evidence in court proceedings. So why would they fear releasing a report if they've got that kind of blanket protection? And why would the Coast Guard, a branch of the mighty U.S. military, be worried about the results of a minor civil case in Florida? That seemed unrealistic. This was an organization with billions of dollars of resources behind them, whole departments full of lawyers. It seemed illogical that they would fear the results of a small civil case – one in which they're not even named.

Yet the fact remains that they are still withholding a relatively straightforward investigation nearly three years later. I have been trying to break that wall down in any way I possibly can. I have spoken to nearly a dozen different people in the Coast Guard trying to get information. I have filed nearly half a dozen freedom of information requests – all of which have been denied. I have appealed those denials and to this point have heard nothing. I have tried to use back channels and off-the-record conversations to get some kind of information. In every single case I have been stymied. Possibly the Coast Guard would be happy if the whole

Stewart case went away – especially if they were aware that their con-clusions might be based on shaky evidence. It wouldn't be inconceivable that they would avoid that fact becoming public by tying the report up in their bureaucracy. A report never released is a report that's never criti-cized. The best off-the-record information I can get is that the report was completed in the fall of 2017. It was sent to regional headquarters where it languished for an unknown period of time. It was eventually passed on to headquarters in Washington, D.C. Somewhere along the line, some authority has chosen to send it back for further work – at least once and possibly twice. What limbo it's lost in now is anybody's guess.

CHAPTER 14

It's a cliché. Almost. Americans are litigious. They sue each other for the slightest transgressions. There seems to be a feeling among some Americans that compensation is some divine right, due even in the most bizarre of circumstances, a feeling that without financial compensation the incident can never be dealt with properly. Many might remember the classic case of the woman who spilled hot coffee in her lap and then sued the fast food outlet for making their coffee too hot. Surprisingly, she won. She eventually lost on appeal, but many of those bizarre financial awards stand.

The Stewart family is not American. They're from Canada. Yet within a couple of months of their son's death they launched a civil action in Florida for negligence. This surprised me for a number of reasons. There wasn't a hurry to file a case. The family had up to two years to file. So why the hurry? Secondly, the investigation into what happened to their son had just begun. No conclusion about the accident had as yet been drawn. Why not wait to see what the investigations turned up? Finally, when I spoke with the Stewarts they were adamant that their only concern was to find out what happened to their son. They never wanted this kind of accident to happen to someone else's child. They've made public statements about this position, Brian Stewart stating, "At this point in time, we're trying to make sure no one ever dies the way Rob died. There's no reason for it, there's no reason for that ever to happen to somebody." But it seemed to me that if they wanted to find out what really happened to their son, if they wanted all the parties to be speaking candidly and sharing what they knew, then launching a lawsuit was not a logical way to proceed. In fact, logically, a lawsuit would have the opposite effect: the moment lawyers and courts became involved, anyone who might have talked was probably going to "lawyer up" and say nothing. So the lawsuit seemed counterintuitive to me, though David Goodhue wasn't the least surprised: "I would anticipate something like this happening, given his status, that there would be a lawsuit."

The Stewarts initially focused their negligence lawsuit against two parties – Peter Sotis and Horizon Divers. Goodhue summed up their position: "The complaint says that Horizon was responsible for Rob since it was their … boat and crew that took him out there. They took his eye off him when there was trouble.… Peter Sotis, the complaint focuses on him because, again, he was the one who trained Rob on the rebreather equipment and basically, he was not prepared to do that kind of dive and the amount of dives that he did that day." The Stewarts announced their lawsuit by holding a press conference at the Miami offices of the Haggard Law Firm, a high-powered group of lawyers they'd engaged to represent them. Surrounded by posters of Rob Stewart's films and copies of his books and DVDs, along with coloured charts to highlight the major points of their case, Michael Haggard hammered home his key points: Sotis and Horizon Divers were negligent and that's why Rob Stewart died. Haggard began the press conference with an overview of what they believed were the "facts." Haggard began by stating, "The world lost one of this generation's true heroes in Rob, in Florida, during a totally preventable diving incident. Unfortunately, what the world doesn't know is how *preventable* and how *reckless* the activity, not only on that day, was by Add Helium, a company out of Fort Lauderdale, and Horizon Divers, a dive operation out of Key Largo, but also in the months before, in the training of Rob Stewart, really what amounted to a *fraudulent inducement* to get him to use certain equipment and training that *violated* every standard in the dive industry."

The statement was chock full of allegations that were unproven in a court, or by any official investigation, for that matter. It was language designed to attract media attention to their case: words like "fraudulent inducement" and "preventable," "reckless" and "violated every standard" begged conclusions that of course the Stewarts' lawyers hope the courts will eventually draw. It's also wise to recall that you can say virtually anything in a complaint filed in a civil case. The allegations only gain credence once the case has been ruled on. Also remember that the standards of proof for a civil case are not as stringent as in a criminal case. In a criminal case you have to prove your allegations beyond a reasonable doubt. In a civil case you just have to prove that the balance of evidence is in your favour. Hence, in the O.J. Simpson case, he was found not guilty in the criminal case, but guilty in the civil case launched against him by the families of the victims.

Lawyer Michael Haggard continued at the press conference, laying out more of their case:

> Rob Stewart and his company hired Add Helium to teach him to dive with what's called a rebreather apparatus. Oftentimes, we think about scuba diving as open circuit scuba diving, where you release bubbles into the water. Rebreathers are closed circuit dive machines, which means that you breathe in oxygen and that that oxygen is reused after carbon dioxide is scrubbed out of it. And you can stay under the water longer, you can go to greater depths, and you don't release bubbles, so you can imagine for military operations, it's very useful because you can go undetected, and if you are the world's number one underwater photographer and film-maker, like Rob Stewart was, it's essential, it can be great for filming sharks and other species underwater at great depths, for longer periods of time, and that's why he *wanted to be trained* in such a, in such an apparatus.

That last statement was a bit of a misdirect. Stewart and Cahill didn't just "want to be trained." They had been very aggressively seeking out someone who would supply them with these devices at a reduced price and train them quickly so they could do the deep dives they wanted on the *Queen of Nassau*.

In fact, according to David Concannon, in May 2016, Stewart had already unsuccessfully approached one diving organization about providing them with equipment and training – Lamar Hires of Dive Rite equipment: "Stewart asked him to sponsor the movie and provide rebreathers, and Lamar said, you're crazy, you're gonna end up just like Wes Skiles. Sorry, but I just went through this ordeal, you can't film on a rebreather if you don't know what you're doing and if you haven't done it in a while. I appreciate that you dove on a Draeger semi-closed in your first film but this is a whole new animal and you're just not, I'm just not gonna help you die like my friend Wes." Skiles was one of the pioneers of cave diving and underwater photography. He died in a rebreather-related accident. His family sued, suggesting the rebreather was faulty. They lost the case. I checked with Lamar Hires about Concannon's statement and he confirmed what he'd said, adding, "I told [Stewart] he needed a couple of hundred hours on the rebreather before he filmed." Hires felt that Stewart was "moving too fast" to use a rebreather and film at the same time. Yet court filings show that, undeterred by this first refusal, Brock Cahill approached a second rebreather manufacturer. He wrote to Paul Revo, the head of the company that made the rebreathers Stewart ultimately used. Cahill asked for sponsorship and said:

> We wondered if you would join us and consider sponsoring part of this mission? might you please give us a smoking deal, or your cost, on a couple of systems? over the next year we will be filming the most unusual and endangered sharks in our oceans, to illuminate and endear people to the beauty of these fish, and turn the tides of shark consumption toward conservation. earlier this week upon completion of a shoot in the bahamas with oceanic whitetips, we toured through florida on a quest for rebreathers. for the next shoots we know that we are going to need the capabilities of CCR. after lumbering through trials and considerations of a couple other systems, yesterday on the way out through ft. lauderdale, we met peter and he showed us the rEvo. we were smitten! wow. if you can find a way to help us out, in return, we can offer the prominent inclusion of the gear in the film, and potentially with the right agreement, a brilliantly shot trailer featuring the rEvo for your marketing uses and mass distribution through our channels.

There's no doubt that Stewart and Cahill were determined to use rebreathers to dive the *Queen of Nassau*. Given how persistent Cahill and Stewart were about finding someone to help them with this, it's a little challenging to accept Haggard's other point that Sotis had been involved in a "fraudulent inducement" to get them to use his gear. If there was any "inducement" involved, it came from Cahill and Stewart, not Sotis.

Haggard continued to promote his case at the press conference by giving a play by play of how the whole rebreather training experience was conducted: "Unfortunately, in the training of Rob Stewart, he met Peter Sotis and Dr. Claudia Sotis, who are the owners of Add Helium, and during that training, they rushed Rob's training and he barely completed the third level course that would take him below 200 feet on this new apparatus that he was using." Of interest in that statement was that it's a kind of "half-empty" view of Stewart's training. Haggard brushed over the fact that Stewart and Cahill had already successfully completed two courses. Haggard said, "He barely completed the third level course." Yet the course that I completed with Add Helium involved rigorous training – four days of non-stop work from morning to night. And that's a schedule based on the fact that I'm already a very experienced diver, as was Stewart. According to Sotis, Stewart did his first course on the re-breather in the summer of 2016, a second more advanced course in the fall of 2016 and the third and final advanced course in the winter of 2017. That meant Stewart had anywhere between 12 and 15 days of training on the device. Now it's true he didn't have a lot of dives in between the courses, but nonetheless, Stewart was not the neophyte being portrayed at the press conference. Haggard continued:

> They went down to the Keys on January 30th and on January 31st, and on January 31st, Rob completed two dives to 225 feet, to a shipwreck called the Queen of Nassau, to try to film the saw-fish. Those dives lasted over an hour, each one of them, well over an hour, and those were the two planned dives that day. When they got back to the boat, the conditions weren't favorable, they didn't find the shark. *Peter Sotis and the Horizon Dive captain* decided that they had to get a $15 grappling hook that was hooked on to the Queen of Nassau, and a rope and a buoy at the top of the water, and that they needed to get this $15 piece of equipment. Dr. Claudia Sotis, a safety diver from Add Helium, was tired and couldn't dive any longer, so Peter Sotis turned to Rob Stewart, his student, and said, hey, let's go for another 225 foot five. There was no dive plan for this dive, there was no new equipment used, there were no oxygen tanks added, and the dive instructor that had this student's life entrusted to him, took him on a third, unprecedented dive to 220 feet depth to get a $15 piece of equipment.

This statement contained multiple questionable "facts." For a start, Claudia Sotis didn't go down for the third dive because her dry suit had flooded earlier in the day. It happens from time to time with dry suits, and when it does, you not only get cold as the water seeps in, but if the suit floods completely you can drown. It would have been extreme folly for Claudia Sotis to go in the water with a leaking suit. She wasn't tired, she was being a safe diver. Haggard also suggested that Peter Sotis invited Stewart along for the third dive. But recall, Sotis vehemently denied he asked Stewart to come along. He claimed Stewart volunteered. Claudia backed that statement, as did the crew on board the *Pisces*. Once again Haggard was presenting his "truth" to support the Stewarts' case, and nothing more. The final factual anomaly was that Haggard suggested that the divers, for some unstated reason, needed "new equipment." Without new equipment, he suggested, the dive involved some kind of increased risk. I have no idea what Haggard was talking about. If the rebreathers had sufficient oxygen in their tanks and their carbon dioxide scrubbers had not reached their limit then no new equipment was needed for the third dive. In fact that was ultimately proven to be the case. The two divers made it down to the wreck and back to the surface after the third dive without running out of air. The NEDU report found no fault with the rebreathers. It wasn't a "new equipment" issue that caused Stewart's death.

Ultimately Haggard comes to the main point of the Stewarts' legal action. He was setting up a negligence argument when he stated, "They came up much quicker than they did on the previous dives. Their decompression profiles were reduced by the dive instructor. They came up in less than 10 minutes." The first point, Haggard suggested, was that Peter Sotis gave his students unsound information on how to conduct the dive ("their decompression schedules were reduced by their instructor"). He also suggested that

> in a highly unprecedented move, the dive instructor swam to the boat first, leaving his student, Rob Stewart, in the open water. Peter Sotis got on the boat and immediately collapsed due to a lack of oxygen, fell to the ground, had to have oxygen administered by his wife, Dr. Claudia Sotis. In the mass confusion of him passing out on the boat, no one, no one from that boat, from Horizon Divers, from Add Helium, kept an eye on Rob Stewart. As you might imagine, he was using the same gas mixtures that Peter Sotis was using, did the same exact three dives that day as Peter Sotis did. There was one difference between the two. One

was safely on board the boat and one was in the open water. It's at that point that Rob sank and disappeared.

Haggard's second point: Peter Sotis clawed his way on to the boat leaving Rob Stewart to die. In so many words, that's the essence of his statement. Again, selective facts slant the argument. Note that Haggard described Sotis as Stewart's "instructor." But in all the correspondence setting up the dive, Sotis was asked by Cahill to join the expedition as a safety diver, not an instructor. So while it is protocol for instructors to allow students to board first, Sotis maintained he wasn't acting in that capacity. Additionally, why Sotis collapsed was still a matter of debate. It might have been a lack of oxygen, it might have been bubbles on the brain caused by decompression, it might even have been carbon dioxide buildup. Haggard was correct, however, in saying that the two men surfaced more quickly on this dive than on previous dives and that may have been one of the critical factors: more on that later.

Haggard also chose the press conference to play a little hardball with Sotis' reputation, explaining that Rob Stewart

> hired a company that was owned by a convicted felon, as Peter Sotis was convicted of a jewelry heist in Naples, Florida, never disclosed to Rob Stewart and his family or his company. He did not know that Peter Sotis was being investigated by the FBI, the Department of Commerce, and the Homeland Security Department of the United States of America, for selling multiple rebreathers and underwater propulsion vehicles to a confirmed Libyan militant. Peter Sotis was warned by the FBI and the Dept. of Commerce to not do this and he did it anyways, and he's under investigation for that at this time.

What was interesting about this statement was that nobody at the press conference asked what I believe was the most important question: What relevance does a criminal conviction Peter Sotis had from 20 years ago have to the current accident? Sotis served his sentence and built a multi-million dollar business, and he'd had no problems with the law other than a couple of speeding tickets. So what was Michael Haggard suggesting? Was he implying that Sotis' previous convictions somehow speak to a criminal mind predisposed to negligence? He did suggest that

Sotis used "fraudulent" means to con Rob Stewart into working with him, so was he now suggesting Sotis possessed criminal tendencies that might include negligence leading to manslaughter? All of which left me a little mystified as to the possible relevance of this fact. It's a headline grabber for sure, and many of the online trolls made a lot of noise about this early conviction, but again they never really explained what relevance they thought it had, other than "see, he's a bad guy" and that anyone with those low moral standards is capable of anything.

Haggard ended his press conference with this final bullet point:

> And maybe most importantly, Rob Stewart did not know that the diving instructor, the company that he trusted, the company that he was allowing to be filmed along with his documentary, promotional materials for this company, that Peter Sotis was manipulating the gas levels on the dive computer to accomplish more aggressive decompression profiles because in his words, he was the best in the business. He knew more than any of the standards that govern rebreathers in the scuba industry across the world. And these dive compression profiles and these gas mixtures are currently being investigated not only by the coroner's office in Monroe County and the Monroe County Sheriff's Office, but the United States Navy, at this time.

But Haggard's contention was not supported by what Rob Stewart's video footage showed. I've mentioned the footage before. It showed the group starting their day with an extensive discussion about the dive profile. They ran though the dive, plugging into their computers what depth they're going to be working at, what bottom times they'll have, what gradient factor they'll use and, yes, what their gas mixture will be. Sotis was clearly the lead diver during this briefing, but he was fastidious when he ran through all the relevant factors that the divers needed to know for the deep dives. In fact they run the whole briefing twice in order to allow the cameraperson to get some reverse angles. Stewart adjusted his own computer. The footage doesn't show Sotis touching it. Now remember, Stewart and Cahill had already completed two courses in technical diving. They'd done the theory and most of the dives for a third course. So was Haggard suggesting that after weeks of training, Stewart, who was programming his own computer, was unaware of what information he was inputting and what that meant for the dive? After one course, I was aware of what those numbers signified. If I hadn't been happy about the numbers Sotis' instructor gave me, I wouldn't have used them.

Haggard ended his media conference with a final statement of outrage: "This was a tragic accident waiting to happen and it has robbed not only the Stewart family of their son but all of us of someone whose sole intent was to save our oceans, which in turn would save all of us. And this recklessness and this dangerous training and operation of Add Helium and Horizon Divers clearly caused this incident and we intend to prove that through this case and keep Rob's mission alive because it is that important."

He then turned the event over to Rob Stewart's parents Brian and Sandra, who continued to pour out further outrage to the media in support of their case. Brian Stewart recapped the point about Sotis not acting appropriately as an instructor,

> and to take your eyes off of the diver in the water, when he's the student and the instructor's on board, is just unimaginable. We're divers, Rob got his diving the same time we did, when he was 13, he started diving and we started diving with him then and we know the rules. I mean you don't, as an instructor, you never leave your student in the water. The self-interest of Peter Sotis is the reason Rob's dead right now. It's all about him. And even from Horizon Divers' perspective, not having eyes on the water, of a diver, when you're the dive boat operator, that's your responsibility, it's just unimaginable.

Brian Stewart also took the moment to point out how critical his son's work had been to the environmental movement: "less than 1/10 of 1% of the world's population actually dive, so you've got about six million divers in the world, they're the only ones that see what Rob saw." Stewart wrapped up his statement with an assertion that the only outcome they were interested in was that this never happen to anyone else. Not everyone accepted that assertion. David Goodhue summed up what many feel: "I'm sure with every lawsuit, it is about money." He noted that diving lawsuits can often be worth millions of dollars in damages if negligence is proven and adds, "Dive companies in general, take on a tremendous amount of risk taking people out diving, and especially on a dive such as this, such a dangerous dive. Hundreds of feet down, there's a tremendous amount of risk and I'm sure they're very worried about how much money they're going to have to pay out."

Since that media conference the lawsuit has been grinding through the courts at a glacial pace. It's been shunted between State Court to Federal Court and then back to State Court. The Stewarts have revised their complaint three times. In fact, just prior to the two-year anniversary of their son's death, and prior to the deadline for naming new parties in the complaint, they filed a new one. This one, some sources say, revealed what might be a major motivation for the case. They've expanded who was named in the action – adding crewperson Robert Steele, boat captain Dave Wilkerson and most importantly, those with the deepest pockets, the rebreather manufacturer, rEvo, and their parent company. They've also made it clear they're going for big dollars when they said they want reimbursement for

> the past and future pain and suffering of Sandra and Brian Stewart; The past and future cost of therapy and mental health treatment for Sandra and Brian Stewart resulting from their son's death; Loss of the care, maintenance, support, services, companionship, advice, counsel, inheritance and other reasonable contributions of pecuniary and non-pecuniary value that Sandra and Brian Stewart would have otherwise received during Plaintiffs' decedents life had it not been for his untimely, tragic and wrongful death; The expense of funeral arrangements arising from the injury and death of Plaintiffs' decedent; The prospective net accumulations of the Estate of ROBERT STEWART; and Any and all other damages that the applicable law allows.

When the Stewarts started asking for any money Rob Stewart might have made during his life and support they might have received in their old age, it suggested that Goodhue may have had a point and that the focus of this lawsuit now included financial considerations, not just the noble cause of ensuring "this never happened to anyone else again."

The revised complaint also inadvertently created another interesting angle to the lawsuit. Once rEvo were named as parties, then lawyer David Concannon came fully into the picture. He brought a more aggressive stance to the table, starting by turning the negligence allegations on their head: "Cahill and Sharkwater Productions arranged the private charter of the Pisces with HORIZON." His bottom line was that if anyone is to blame for Stewart's death, why not look at the people who organized this dangerous shoot? Brock Cahill was the primary "shaker and mover" behind the whole event, according to Concannon: "Brock Cahill set up the charter, Brock Cahill had all the communications with rEvo. Brock Cahill, you know, was integral in finding Sotis. It was Brock and Rob and Brock was doing all the work, Rob, Rob was kind of like the boss and Cahill was, I don't know that he was the employee but he was certainly, he was the guy that, he was initially supposed to be an associate producer on this, but he was the guy doing the legwork."

Concannon said if Rob Stewart's death was anything other than an accident, then Cahill should hold a certain amount of liability. He went further and pointed the finger at the Stewarts' own production company, "because you can see communications with Sharkwater Productions to Horizon saying, you know they're diving rebreathers, right? So, you've got the production company is aware of the technical aspects of the charters as well." Oddly, Concannon suggested that Sotis' liability was limited: "Sotis comes late to the party but he didn't have any involvement in that other than meeting the boat and that's, I think, very, very interesting, that's all on Horizon and Cahill and Sharkwater Productions." In fact Concannon believed the case obfuscated the real matter of who was at fault when they tried to direct it towards Peter Sotis: "He was the convenient fall guy. I think that, look, number one, he's not there, Number two, he is, to be kind, people have mixed opinions about Peter, some negative, some positive." When it comes time for trial, Concannon said, "I wanted to hold the mirror up to them. You're the producers of this film, you're the ones, you're the executive producer, you've got the superior responsibility over and above your son, to keep him safe. We're going to have that conversation in this case. They're going to have to look themselves in the mirror and ask what they did wrong, which I'm certain they've done, but they haven't testified to it under oath."

Concannon will build his case around the belief that if any other parties should shoulder some blame, in addition to Cahill and Sharkwater Productions, it should be the dive boat. The skipper of the boat, Dave Wilkerson, said he asked Brock Cahill to keep an eye on Rob when the emergency started, but Concannon said that's just nonsense:

The issue with Cahill and the captain is that the captain should have asked the mate to keep an eye on the passenger, not a passenger to keep an eye on a passenger. Now, it was my understanding that the mate was holding the oxygen bottle for Sotis at that time, while Sotis was being worked on by a doctor. Cahill is more capable of holding an oxygen bottle than he is in rescuing somebody who's out on the water. The mate is supposed to be trained, the mate is supposed to know the boat's procedures, the mate has done the man overboard drills, the mate knows where the, the safety gear is on the boat, so it's the mate's job. So, yeah, so it's another mistake that Wilkerson made.

And he added that the owner of Horizon Divers should have planned the whole expedition better – he knew where his charter was going.

Dawson is the one with the superior knowledge. Dawson's been hired to do a job, take these guys out to a place they've never been, where Dawson knows it and Horizon knows it and nobody else does, that's the thing where Sotis, I think, gets a pass, not a whole pass, an entire pass, but he's never been there, he doesn't know the wreck, he doesn't know the Keys, he doesn't, he can certainly dive to 200 feet on a wreck but he's not the errant, the local, he doesn't have the local knowledge. He doesn't know the currents, he doesn't know the visibility, he doesn't know the wreck, he doesn't know the orientation. He can discover it but he's learning at the same time as the others are learning…. He's not, he's not equipping the vessel…. There's b-roll shot the day before, they didn't have enough rope, they were ill-equipped for that charter, but they didn't think about it in advance. I'm sure Wilkerson just showed up and looked at the schedule and saw that he was going to take the boat out on Caloosa Cove, he was junior captain, so he's, he's not giving any forethought to, I'm gonna need 300 feet of line for the grappling hook and I'm gonna need digital equipment on board the boat, I've got a single 80-cubic foot tank of air, air, for my rescue, for my diver.

Peter Sotis is represented by attorney Neil Bayer. I asked him multiple times to speak with me about the court case, and though he agreed multiple times, he was never available. Meanwhile, the case has stretched on for more than three years and is showing no sign of being resolved. Original trial dates set for the fall of 2017 have been put off time and time again. Multiple motions have been filed and fought. One motion of note was a motion to dismiss filed by rEvo. They pointed out that nowhere in the Stewarts' complaint did they ever indicate *how* rEvo was negligent. It forced the Stewarts to once again file a revised complaint, but the case is by no means a slam dunk for the family.

There have been rumours of negotiations behind the scenes for a settlement, but nothing has been made public. It's very possible this case could stretch on for many more years if it's ever resolved at all. One thing is certain: the case did exactly what many said it would do. It shut down all communication that might have allowed for a quick and easy discovery of what happened to Rob Stewart. Yet despite the legal hurdles, it is possible to piece together what really happened.

CHAPTER 15

After more than two years of research, I'm constantly asked what conclusions I've drawn about what really happened to Rob Stewart. I was reluctant initially to draw any conclusions. In the documentary *The Third Dive: The Death of Rob Stewart*, I laid out the various options and let people make their own minds up. I took some criticism for that approach. But with an additional year or more of work on this investigation, I've decided that it is possible to come to a conclusion. I admit the process has been one in which I've revised my conclusions twice – both times when new information appeared.

On a very simple level, Rob Stewart drowned: most diving deaths are attributed to drowning, because, ultimately, that's what actually kills the person, asphyxiation. So the real question became, what triggered the event that led to the drowning? There are a lot of ways a person can die while diving. Not to be overly simplistic, but you are after all in an alien environment, one in which you can't breathe unaided and have all manner of different physical forces affecting your body. Fortunately it was not that difficult to eliminate most of those causes of death. For example, in this case it was possible to immediately eliminate any biological cause – no poisonous creatures stung him, no large predator attacked him. He and his diving partner, Peter Sotis, saw nothing remotely resembling anything dangerous while they were under the water (the shark Sotis reported seeing was merely curious and swam over to inspect them and then swam away). It's also possible to eliminate the most common cause of drowning while diving. Stewart didn't have a heart attack or some equally serious physical problem that led to a blackout and drowning. The medical examiner eliminated those causes during the autopsy. In fact, Beaver stated that Stewart was in great physical condition. He also stated there were no drugs present that might have led to unconsciousness underwater. I could also eliminate equipment failure or running out of air to breathe. The Navy report provided that information. So the common reasons are out; what's left?

That means it had to be some kind of an effect resulting from changes to the gas he was breathing while diving. But some of those effects can also be eliminated right away. For example, something like nitrogen narcosis might cause a diver to black out or do something foolhardy that would lead to drowning. But that happens to a diver when he or she is deep under the water. Depth causes nitrogen to have a narcotic effect. That effect disappears in shallow water. Recall that both Sotis and Stewart made it back to the surface. The incident that killed Stewart did not happen while he was deep underwater. So nitrogen narcosis was out.

There's a very slim possibility it might have been helium poisoning. Stewart and Sotis were breathing a gas mix that included helium. But that's also virtually impossible as a cause. Recorded instances of helium poisoning have come about as a result of commercial divers breathing high concentrations of helium for days, not a matter of a couple of hours, and at extreme depths – 300–400 feet down. That left me with a narrow range in terms of what could have happened. There were really only four possibilities: hypoxia, or too little oxygen in the breathing mixture; hyperoxia, breathing too rich an oxygen mixture; hypercapnea, breathing air contaminated with carbon dioxide; and decompression sickness, or bubbles being released from the blood and wreaking havoc on the body.

When I set out to try and narrow down those four possibilities, my first thought was to talk with the man who last dived with Rob Stewart – Peter Sotis – and ask him what he thought. I'd already talked with him on several occasions and interviewed him extensively. But when I got him on the phone, his bottom line was, "I have no idea. And I've spent a lot of time, as you can imagine, I've spent a lot of time thinking about it. I've spent a lot of time with my wife in discussing what she observed and the neurological assessments that she did for me when I was going through this event and … we can't find anything that matches that event, which is not unusual. There are many things that happen in diving and we just can't explain them and unfortunately, this is one of them."

In a way Sotis was right. Whatever happened to Stewart does not fit a cookie-cutter mould for any of the final four possibilities. So the question was, which of the four does it most closely resemble? Sotis claimed that after he got on board the boat, he blacked out and for several minutes had no recollection of the events that followed. But he remembered the dive very clearly and was adamant that nothing odd happened during the dive that would signal the oncoming catastrophic event. I asked him about the common denominator – the fact that whatever happened occurred at the same time to both Rob and himself. I wondered what significance that had for him. Sotis said he thought it was pure coincidence:

In the time that I've spent learning about diving and learning about the effects of diving the likelihood of two divers experiencing a simultaneous event would have to be in the millions to one. So I don't believe it's possible. While it sounds plausible to the average person, that something happened to me, something must have happened to Rob, but the likelihood of the same thing happening to both of us at exactly the same time on the same dive is, I'm not sure you could even put a number on, on how unlikely that is. So I don't think whatever happened to me is what happened to Rob.

Sotis claimed he wanted to find out just as badly as anyone else what occurred. His reputation was still on the line. "Something happened to Rob. There's ... no doubt about that.... I'd love nothing better than to at least be able to ... define it down to one particular instance that we both suffered, and then I'd know what happened to me as well." I'm not sure I agree with Peter Sotis about the simultaneous event being pure coincidence. Certainly the medical examiner didn't agree with him and based his entire diagnosis on the fact that the two men had a simultaneous event. Additionally, it's hard to ignore the fact that the two men had made identical dives during the two days – the same depth, the same surfacing rate, the same gas, the same PO_2, everything the same. Dr. Neal Pollock also liked to point out that the fact that Sotis had never encountered such an event before doesn't mean it couldn't happen. Pollock suggested the two men, given the depth and frequency of their dives, were well beyond what research science had conducted on the effects of deep diving.

And that Sotis had no theories about what happened to him didn't mean the trail ran cold. There are a couple of critical clues during the frantic few moments that Stewart was back on the surface after his third dive of the day. Several of the people on board, including Brock Cahill, his friend, say that Rob's loop had fallen out of his mouth. Remember, the loop on a rebreather is what you draw breath from. When you train on a rebreather, you're taught to never take the loop out of your mouth until you're back in the boat. There may be the rare occasion when you have to take it out, and then there is a procedure for doing that. You have to seal the loop with a valve so water won't get into it and then take it out. It's also not taken out because after a long deep dive, you want to be breathing the high concentration of oxygen that you've set your rebreather to give you on the surface to clear out any residual nitrogen in your system. So why did Stewart have the loop out of his mouth? Possibly because he was already experiencing some event when he broke the surface. Reports from some of the people on the boat suggested that Stewart was non-responsive when he was in the water. Repeated calls for him to grab the tag line went unheeded. Add to that there's also no evidence to suggest that Stewart was an incompetent diver who would breach his training protocols about dropping the loop; in fact, quite the contrary, everyone described him as a superb diver. I also noted that during the previous day's diving, the video showed that Stewart followed the protocol with his loop religiously. It stayed in his mouth until he was back on the boat. So I have to conclude that he had already blacked out shortly after hitting the surface and that caused the loop to fall out of his slack mouth. That would coincide with the exact moment that Sotis blacked out on board the boat. If Stewart's loop did fall out of his mouth and he had not inflated his wing, water would pour into the rebreather flooding the counter lungs, and the dead weight of that unit would drag him like an anchor to the bottom. All this wouldn't happen if Stewart inflated his buoyancy device on the surface. So the second question that has to be asked is, did Stewart inflate his wing when he reached the surface after the third dive?

In December 2018, Peter Sotis wanted to see if he could prove that Stewart had not inflated his wing. He found a mannequin that weighed approximately the same as a human male, put a rebreather unit on it and then allowed the unit to flood – first with the wing inflated and then with the wing uninflated. He did this procedure several times, filmed it and invited impartial experts to observe. The results were identical. Every time the wing was inflated, it kept the diver at the surface even when the rebreather flooded. Every time the wing wasn't inflated the

diver went down like a rock. Sotis believed this experiment was con-
clusive proof that Stewart broke one of the rules of diving: when you
surface you inflate your flotation device. Interestingly, the footage shot
by Stewart's cameraperson the day before showed that Stewart did not
inflate his wing at the surface. Now it is possible to be buoyant at the
surface without inflating your wing when you're using a rebreather. The
counter lung in the rebreather will keep you afloat. You can also use the
air in your dry suit to keep afloat, though again, divers are still told to
inflate their buoyancy device. If Stewart followed the same protocols he
had on the previous day, he would not have inflated his wing. If his rebreather flooded he would have been dragged down.

Still, the discussion about his wing only answers the question of what
would have happened after he blacked out. None of that discussion answers the question, what made him black out in the first place? I spoke
to some of the world's leading experts on diving to help me with this.
My first line of inquiry was, could it have been hyperoxia or central nervous system (CNS) oxygen toxicity? Simply put, too much oxygen. I contacted the manager of the diving program at NOAA (National Oceanic
and Atmospheric Administration), Greg McFall. He's a former Navy
diver who's spent the better part of the last 20 years working as a scientific researcher for the likes of the University of North Carolina and
NOAA. He's been involved in the diving world for more than 40 years and
overseen multiple studies on the physiological impact of diving. He was
already familiar with the Stewart case when I contacted him, telling me,
"Their diving was aggressive, we wouldn't do two dives to that depth in
one day." When I asked whether he felt Stewart might have blacked out
from CNS, he was doubtful, saying, "In the thousands and thousands of
dives I've done, I've only every seen it once." He admitted that there are
some medications that increase susceptibility, like Sudafed and some an-
tidepressants, but maintained that the odds "are very remote." He also
pointed out that it's "rare for CNS to occur at or near the surface. It usually happens at depth." Neither Sotis or Stewart experienced any problems at depth. Their incident happened on the surface, where the effects
of water pressure were no longer affecting the oxygen they were breathing. So it would be statistically improbable that both Sotis and Stewart
defied physics and succumbed at the surface to a problem that almost always happens deep underwater. Finally, McFall named off the symptoms

of CNS: tunnel vision, ear ringing, nausea, muscle spasms, anxiety, dizziness and, most importantly, convulsions. "There is usually a seizure first. The body becomes rigid then the body relaxes and that's when the loop could come out of the mouth. If Peter Sotis didn't convulse then that pretty much rules out CNS." Nobody mentioned anything about Sotis having a convulsion. When I spoke with his wife Claudia, a former emergency room physician, she said there were no signs of any convulsions. In McFall's opinion, it wasn't hyperoxia. That reduced the number of possibilities down to three.

The next cause that I wanted to eliminate was hypercapnia, or carbon dioxide poisoning. This was a distinct possibility, particularly when you're using a rebreather. Remember a rebreather "re-uses" the air you breathe by removing the carbon dioxide. But the chemical that does that has a life span, and when it's used up all of its "scrubbing" capability, it stops working. It will only absorb carbon dioxide for a limited number of minutes. In the case of Rob Stewart and Peter Sotis, they were both diving with a state of the art rebreather made by rEvo in Belgium. The twin scrubbers, according to the manual that rEvo gives out with the unit, are rated (with some variation depending on depth and temperature) for around 160 minutes. My first thought on seeing this number in the manual was that I had finally found a viable cause of death. When you add the three dives together that Stewart and Sotis did on that final day, it added up to 209 minutes. That exceeded the recommended time by 49 minutes. But I soon found out that there were a couple of problems with my initial supposition. First of all, rEvo's manual suggested that their timeline was for water that is 4 degrees Celsius. That's pretty cold water. That's going to affect how long the absorbent lasts. According to Shearwater Manufacturing, the company that made Stewart and Sotis' computers, their research on absorbent states, "If you are diving in warm water, the absorbent will be warmer than it would be in cold water. Generally the absorbent is better at removing the CO_2 when it is warm. For instance, diving in 15°C (59°F) water may increase the endurance by 50% compared to the 4°C water where the stated endurance was most likely determined. Diving in 30°C (86°F) water may increase the endurance by another 25 to 40%."

The water temperature on the day of the dives, according to Stewart's computer, was around 22 degrees Celsius – considerably warmer than the 4 degrees mentioned in the rEvo manual. Also, the rating in the rEvo manual was calculated for a depth of 40 metres. Stewart and Sotis went as deep as 67 metres but spent two-thirds of their dive decompressing between 20 and 4 metres. I'd also heard that the time ratings given by rebreather companies were often very conservative, for insurance liability purposes. In other words, they didn't want to get sued for being wrong. In fact I'd heard those dives times could often be double what the manual rating listed.

Fortunately there was a way to take the guesswork out of the whole equation. NEDU, the Navy Experimental Diving Unit that tested the equipment for the medical examiner, ran a series of tests on the carbon dioxide scrubbers in Rob Stewart's rebreather. They recreated the conditions, running three back-to-back dives to a depth of more than 68 metres. They simulated the same breathing rate that rEvo used to calculate its run time on their scrubbers, 1.6 litres per minute. Then they watched to see how long the absorbent material would continue to work properly – keep the amount of carbon dioxide below 0.5 per cent SEV (surface equivalent value). NEDU found that the scrubbers worked effectively for 265 minutes. In fact it wasn't until the 362-minute mark that the carbon dioxide level reached 2.0 % SEV – a level that would likely cause the diver to black out. Brock Cahill stated that both he and Stewart changed their scrubbers the morning of the dive. So if we go by the experiments done by NEDU, Stewart and Sotis had at least 265 minutes on those scrubbers before any kind of problem could be expected, possibly as much as 362 minutes. Sotis and Stewart had a total dive time of 209 minutes. That's a margin of safety of 56 minutes. So it would have been extremely unlikely for Sotis and Stewart to succumb to hypercapnia – they were breathing well-scrubbed air throughout all three of their dives. That left two possible causes – hypoxia and decompression sickness.

I started examining hypoxia – the official cause of blackout listed by medical examiner Dr. Thomas Beaver. In his final report he stated, "Based on the information available to me at this time it is my opinion that both Peter Sotis and Robert Stewart suffered acute hypoxia at the surface. Once Mr. Stewart lost consciousness he lost control of the breathing loop and drowned. Therefore, it is my opinion that the cause of death is best certified as Drowning with the manner of death classified as Accident." I asked Dr. Beaver multiple times about his diagnosis of hypoxia and whether he was absolutely certain about it. He admitted that no one possible diving ailment fit all of the criteria that would allow a definitive explanation. He told me that he came up with his answer by reverting to his medical training: in the absence of a clear cause of death or illness, physicians look at the symptoms and reverse engineer the events to come up with a diagnosis. "In medicine we call it the differential diagnosis, that's my differential and that's how I approach each of those things and can I say 100%? No. I don't think anybody will ever be able to say 100% but I think, in my opinion, it's more weighted towards the hypoxia than it is DCS, just because of that clinical presentation of Peter Sotis." So what symptoms did the two men exhibit for Beaver that pushed him towards hypoxia? He says:

> Both divers have the same dive profile, they're diving the same gear, they've been on the same dive, they come up essentially together, and one diver gets out of the water and on the boat and collapses, passes out, and by his own admission he said, I passed out, those were his words to the coast guard. And the other diver is at the surface and I think he passes out too but he's in the water and there's no rescue, he sinks to the, below the surface. So the diver on the boat provides us with the clinical symptoms of whatever the diver in the water had. So now I've got a really, I've got a window into what happened to the diver in the water that I almost never get, I never get that because usually it's one diver dies and nobody knows why, and all the other divers are fine. But this diver, he got up on the boat, so whatever knocked Peter Sotis out on the boat, we can assume has also knocked Rob Stewart out in the water. So now we look at Peter Sotis and we say what could it be?

Given what Sotis experienced – how quickly he recovered, coupled with the fact that he required no further treatment in a decompression chamber, Beaver concluded that his symptoms most closely resembled hypoxia. But as discussed earlier, there are some problems with that diagnosis. For the divers to succumb to hypoxia, their rebreather units would have to be feeding them a mixture of gas that was very thin on oxygen. Scientist Neal Pollock pointed out that there's a lot of data about the rebreathers Sotis and Stewart used. "You have a great source of documentation and that's the rebreather information … you have a tremendous amount of data about the health of the rebreather units." Pollock pointed out that the rebreathers were extensively tested by NEDU and their findings contradict what Beaver concluded. NEDU found the oxygen sensors, which would tell the divers what they were breathing – five of them in each rebreather – were all working well. It's possible that an oxygen sensor can malfunction, but between Sotis and Stewart they had a total of ten oxygen sensors at work, and the odds that all ten would simultaneously fail are beyond belief.

So, if we accept that those oxygen sensors were working, then the next step is to look at the information they provided about the gas that Sotis and Stewart were breathing. Each man had two computers. Each computer was logging the oxygen levels being fed to the men. All of those computers agree on one point. The partial pressure of the oxygen that the two men were being supplied never dipped to critical levels. Stewart and Sotis were not breathing a hypoxic mixture. Even Beaver acknowledged that the data troubled him: "It's part of the reason I won't say 100% hypoxia, because there could be ... there is some argument against hypoxia and that does argue against it." At the end of day, Beaver went with hypoxia because, while it wasn't perfect, it was the closest fit to the whole mystery. The problem is that NEDU's information showed that hypoxia was physically impossible. That was later confirmed when Shearwater took the divers' computers and downloaded the diagnostic level in the computers, showing the minute-by-minute sampling the computer was doing on the gas. Even on a minute-by-minute level, the gas never became hypoxic. That effectively eliminated hypoxia as a cause of blackout and left the only alternative as decompression sickness.

You may recall that earlier I talked about DCS. It occurs when divers come up too fast. If the diver ascends slowly, the body will release that absorbed gas without any problem. If the diver comes up too quickly that gas will form into bubbles, release them into the bloodstream, the joints and the lungs and, depending on where those bubbles travel, cause a huge amount of damage to the body. They can block blood flow, travel to the heart and stop it, get trapped in joints and cause enormous pain, they can travel to the brain and cause the equivalent of a stroke. The symptoms of a diver suffering from DCS vary a great deal depending on where the bubbles form. If they've formed in the surface blood vessels near the skin then the symptom can be a simple rash. If they appear in the joints then pain and stiffness are often the most usual symptoms. But the symptoms get a little trickier if the bubbles form elsewhere. Cerebral Decompression Sickness, or DCS, in the brain "may produce almost any symptom: headache or visual disturbance, dizziness, tunnel vision, tinnitus (buzzing or ringing in the ears) partial deafness, confusion, disorientation, emotional, even psychotic symptoms, paralysis, and unconsciousness."

The treatment for a diver showing signs of DCS is to get them breathing pure oxygen as soon as possible and transport them to a decompression chamber. That's one sticking point in this being accepted universally as the cause of why Stewart drowned, because when Sotis started showing symptoms on the boat, he was given oxygen and he recovered within minutes. He did not require any treatment in a chamber. At first look, that fact made it counterintuitive to say that this must have been DCS. But Dr. Neal Pollock disagrees. He is firmly convinced that both divers suffered from a DCS hit of a very specific kind. He calls it a transient neurological decompression hit: "They were able to come up hard and fast. And my belief is that based on the evidence we have and what we know didn't fail, the most likely explanation is that that fast ascent on the third dive caused a bubble formation that was affecting their [central nervous system]. So their brains were affected by fresh bubble formation and that was demonstrated in the psycho-motor changes that Peter demonstrated when he climbed back on the boat and then collapsed." Little wonder they blacked out, says Pollock, given the dive profiles of the two divers: "They were diving very aggressively and repeatedly, and it's very foreseeable, very reasonable to imagine that they would get a transient flash of bubbles in the brain that could cause the symptoms that were present in Peter. And we don't see it usually because most people don't go up as quickly as they did." What Pollock suggested was that the aggressive ascent made by Sotis and Stewart on that third dive of the day released bubbles from the soft tissue of their brains and caused them to experience momentary confusion and blackout.

When you examine the surface ascent rates used by Stewart and Sotis on that final dive, that may be as close to a definitive piece of information as we get in this case. They rose at 75 feet per minute. The standard ascent rate from a dive shouldn't exceed 30 feet per minute. There are some divers who still use an ascent rate of 60 feet per minute, but most abandoned that standard years ago. Sotis and Stewart were rising at more than double the accepted rate of ascent. In fact, in two days of diving from extreme depths, Stewart only surfaced once at the accepted rate of ascent. On every other dive he surfaced more quickly, at speeds ranging from 38 to 48 feet per minute. The accumulated effect of that practice was, to my knowledge, beyond where science had conducted any experimentation. Yet there was still the matter of Sotis not having to do to a decompression chamber. I asked Pollock how to account for that fact. He said that was easily explained: "I think that the reason [the DCS bubbles] were transient was because they affected the brain and the brain is so well profused and has such a good blood flow, that they were able to clear that excess inert gas fairly quickly. So, it may have been that it was a limited amount of inert gas, that it was at just the right time and big enough bolus that it affected the brain, but then the blood cleared it out." He's suggesting that because the brain is a soft tissue and has such a rich supply of oxygenated blood, that any small bubbles that formed causing the men to black out would have been quickly flushed out. Pollock continued his argument by pointing out the circumstances of the dives Sotis and Stewart performed: "You have guys who are lying to their computers, they're doing a very rapid ascent, I am not at all surprised that they're getting symptoms. It is a little bit surprising that they're transient but here's why to me it makes sense that they're affecting the brain tissue. The brain is fairly quickly flushed, so that is about the only way you can explain this situation."

I researched neurological decompression sickness and found virtually no studies about the subject outside of one letter to the editor in *The Lancet* medical journal back in 1989. It suggested a link between neurological DCS and patent foramen ovale, PFO (a hole between the two chambers of the heart that some people have that occasionally in divers allows gas to travel between the two sides of the heart and get unrestricted access to the brain). It could have been relevant in this case if one or both divers had a PFO. Sotis told me he's never been diagnosed with one. But Pollock dismisses the need for a diver to have a PFO in order to succumb to a neurological DCS hit. He says the science has evolved a great deal since 1989, and they now know that bubbles can travel to the brain in a number of ways.

Given the evidence that's available to this point, Pollock's analysis of neurological DCS seemed to be the most likely explanation. Though there are some challenges to having neurological DCS fit the situation, it checks off most of the boxes. The two men were diving aggressively for two days. By the time they had completed their third dive on day two, they had put in five dives to below 200 feet for extended periods. Their computers were set to allow them a very aggressive surfacing protocol – one within the limits of safe diving, but only just. The two divers had also adjusted their helium levels to avoid any additional decompression penalty, which some maintain could have serious consequences, but there is also research to suggest that the so-called helium penalty (adding extra decompression time because the diver has helium mixed into their breathing gas) is a bit of a myth. I looked at a NEDU study from 2015 that suggested there was no difference in decompression penalties when divers reduced the amount of helium they were breathing. But Pollock argues there are *other* factors that the helium penalty covers that offer an extra margin of safety: "It's possible the helium penalty may be high for helium but I also think it covers a multitude of other sins that dive computers don't consider. For instance, what dive computer knows how hard you've been working? None. What dive computer knows your thermal status? None. What knows your age, your fatness, your fitness, your, whether you are well hydrated or poorly hydrated? Not a single computer knows any of those things. So that helium penalty is protective, if not for the helium but for the multitude of other things that make us less than perfect." In other words, any additional safety margin that could have helped the two men avoid some kind of problem with decompression sickness had been shaved to the bone. It's quite possible that they could have completed the day and had no problems if they had not done the third dive. But once that dive was involved in the equation then they were entering into some very risky territory.

After working on this investigation for more than two years, I believe that a DCS hit caused Rob Stewart to black out, lose control of his loop, flood his rebreather and subsequently be dragged down the bottom and drown. But what caused Rob Stewart to drown was a little more complicated that that. That's because the most important question to ask about the death of Rob Stewart isn't what happened that caused him to black out and drown; rather, I think the critical question to ask is *why* it happened. I'm not just playing at semantics with that statement. I really believe, to quote an old cliché, that the events leading up to Stewart's death were "the perfect storm" of mismanaged plans and personalities that cascaded towards the final events that led to his death.

CHAPTER 16

The "storm" began to gather the moment Stewart made the decision to dive on the *Queen of Nassau* to film sawtooth sharks. The dive meant descending to a depth of more than 200 feet and required extensive technical experience. On top of that he was intending to film using a rebreather – by all accounts a double skill that required hundreds of hours of practice. Add all of that together and Stewart was creating an enormous challenge for himself, one considerably beyond his expertise.

I tried to set up the same dive. I thought that having a shot of a diver descending to and circling around the *Queen of Nassau* would be a great addition to my documentary. I've been in the television business for more than 30 years and I've been a technical diver for more than ten so I knew that this wouldn't be very easy to accomplish. I approached this setup with a great deal of care. The dive was beyond my skill level and beyond the level of my director of photography, who was doing some underwater filming at shallow depths for the project. So my next thought was, who is certified and experienced at filming in those depths? I contacted three of the best underwater cinematographers and exploration divers in the world: Jill Heinerth, Becky Kagan Schott and David Ulloa. Jill was not available, but I did get quotes from Becky and David: it would have cost thousands of dollars a day to do the dive; multiple days to do practice runs on getting to the wreck; and hiring professional safety divers, who were experienced at working with cinematographers at depth. Those were just the basic requirements that I would need to provide to hire either one of these people. These two were some of the best divers and shooters in the world, with a huge amount of experience, and yet they planned this shoot as if they were going to do a moon walk. Ultimately the cost was so prohibitive that I chose to give up the shot. It would have cost the production too much money and I couldn't do it myself. Yet Stewart and Cahill thought they could do it all on their own – with no experienced underwater filmmakers who knew rebreathers – take a couple of courses, bring in a totally inexperienced safety diver and penetrate below 200 feet using rebreathers and film sharks. You may recall that Lamar Hires, CEO of Dive Rite and a hugely experienced rebreather diver, had told Stewart, he claimed, that he and Cahill should spend 200 or more hours learning to use the rebreather before they tried to simultaneously film. They ignored that advice and threw themselves into planning the dives.

Court records indicate that the logistics of setting up the training, getting the gear in place and organizing the dive for Rob Stewart's shoot were mostly left to Brock Cahill and a producer with Sharkwater Productions named Karen Shaw. Their email chain can be found in court filings in the Stewart civil case. It showed a very fast setup time between when they started contacting Sotis for training, rEvo for gear and finally Horizon Divers for a boat charter: less than a year from start to finish. This technical setup was completed by Brock Cahill, who had virtually no experience in the film business and, prior to his training with Add Helium, did not hold any certifications in technical diving. "He was the guy doing the legwork," according to Concannon, "at the time, if he's not an employee of Sharkwater and he's got personal responsibility on his own right, if he is an employee of Sharkwater, we need to know that, we don't know that yet, we'll find out in discovery, but he's got personal culpability. He is the guy that set up the charter, he's the guy that arranged for, you know, or at least he's, he did it equally with Rob Stewart."

Concannon and others believe the timeline to train, get new equipment and organize a series of deep dives was rushed. Certainly that seemed patently obvious on the training side of the equation. Learning to do decompression diving to any depth isn't just a matter of taking a course. You have to work your skills, and practise relentlessly to make those skills not just something you're vaguely familiar with but something that's part of your muscle memory. Every time I go for a dive, regardless of the depth, I review the basic safety drills associated with technical diving – air sharing with my buddy, value drills to shut down a malfunctioning tank, running a safety line, releasing marker bags to the surface, etc. etc. I do this so that if some kind of emergency happens then my response is calm and automatic. In fact, just recently, I had to put those skills into effect. While diving in Howe Sound in British Columbia,

I got down to around 80 feet and my face mask fell apart. I couldn't see, and opening my eyes meant they were washed by salt water. I was forced to do an ascent to the surface completely blind. But I've practised a similar drill in cave training using blackout masks, so it was no big deal. I slowly ascended, signalled the boat, they gave me a new mask and I went back down and continued the dive. That could have gone very differently if I hadn't remained calm and confident in my abilities. I'm not suggesting that the scale of my emergency was similar to what Stewart and Cahill could have encountered, only that you have to work technical diving skills relentlessly before you're ready to pick up a camera.

Cahill and Stewart also didn't have a lot of deep diving experience on their rebreathers. Though they had taken a number of courses, I can only find one dive to the kind of depths they were working at with their film gear on the *Queen of Nassau*. In fact, Stewart only had 39 dives logged on his computer when he headed out to do the filming – insignificant experience when it came to making multiple dives on multiple days to below 200 feet with a camera. But those kinds of challenges didn't dissuade the two men from proceeding with the plan. The whole expedition, in fact, had an aura of hubris surrounding it – no surprise to the people who knew Rob Stewart. Fellow shark enthusiast Chris Harvey-Clark had a good working relationship with Stewart. He watched Stewart while on an anti-finning mission in Cape Verde off the coast of Africa. He watched him penetrate the secure parts of a dock while they were looking for evidence of finning:

> I don't think Rob had a lot of fear in him. You know, every situation I saw where people might be wary, he would just plough ahead. He was, he definitely, was somebody who I wouldn't call him brave, I just don't think he was a fearful person. I think he'd probably faced death a few times in his life and realized, what's the worst that can happen here? We get ejected from the dock, maybe we get arrested, something like that. I think he weighed the odds there and just, if he even did, I think he just went ahead and did it. He was a go-for-it kind of guy.

In fact Harvey-Clark thinks that attitude was the double-edged sword that made Stewart the success he was but, by necessity, a risk taker. "I think he took calculated risks like we all do, like I've done, certainly in the studies I've done where we're working with dangerous animals in the water, but you do all the things you need to do." That's also the assessment of Stewart's environmental companion in arms, Sea Shepherd President Paul Watson. He completely agreed with Harvey-Clark, saying, "If you believe in something enough, then that just comes naturally. I don't think, I don't think you really have to even think about it." Watson went further and added that without that hubris people like him and Rob Stewart would never achieve what they set out to do.

You don't think of the costs, actually. I mean that never even enters your mind. When I'm on a ship and I'm engaged in a confrontation, you're in a completely different mindset. What you're doing is you're responding to the actions but you're not really thinking about the consequences. And so this way, it's actually, it gives you the ability to be effective because you're not ... you're not diverted by thoughts of failure or thoughts of this is going to happen, that's going to happen, it's all very ... right in the present, it's right in the present. And I actually find that to be one of the most comfortable experiences that I've ever had, when I'm in those situations, because there's no, there's really no doubts and you just focus on that one thing.

Watson added, as a final thought, that if you can't conquer that fear of death, then you're in the wrong business:

If you're not afraid of dying, you can do absolutely anything you put your mind to. That's the one great, you know, barrier to achieving anything....

Interviewer: Do you think Rob had lost his fear of death?

Watson: I think ... yeah, I don't think that he was concerned about that.

I believe that the real tragedy in this accident is that it was almost a foregone conclusion. When Stewart's "go for it" attitude met what was a loosely planned and extremely dangerous series of dives, then the result was inevitable without a great deal of luck. So at the end of the day, what really killed Rob Stewart? As in many catastrophic underwater accidents, it's never one problem, it's a cascade of problems: The first problem may be small, a diver has a problem with his mask. He starts to deal with it and perhaps becomes entangled in some line. Now the problem is growing. The diver starts to panic, drops his light, now the problem is becoming life threatening. What started as a simple problem cascades out of control, and unless you can really hold your shit together, it can quite easily kill you. In Stewart's case his death began with a filming expedition that was beyond his capability; it continued with the adoption of technology for diving that should have taken years to master, not months; it cascaded when Stewart picked up his camera and thought he could dive and film at the same time; it reached a peak with a series of dives that were beyond the limit of Cahill and Stewart's expertise. It finally ended when Stewart made the decision to make the third dive. That pushed both Stewart and Sotis into territory beyond the knowledge of science, where a fast ascent and a neurological DCS hit caused them to black out. In Stewart's case he blacked out in the water, dropped his loop, flooded his rebreather and was dragged down to the bottom to drown.

No one thing killed Rob Stewart. A whole series of bad decisions killed him.

One final note on Stewart's diving partner Peter Sotis. You may recall that he'd gotten a nasty note from the Department of Commerce telling him not to ship rebreathers to a Middle Eastern man named Mohammad Zaghab who had connections to Libya. Sotis claimed the whole issue was a tactic set up to discredit him by a former business partner. He was certain that it had all blown over. It hadn't. In October 2019, the Department of Commerce laid charges which claimed "no entity or individual appearing in this Indictment obtained the necessary license from the Department of Commerce to export rebreathers to Libya." That doesn't sound too bad, failing to get a licence to export some goods. But what's worse is that the U.S. federal government is claiming this wasn't just some accident that involved the shipment having been sent before Sotis and his manager got the email telling them to hold the goods purchased by Zaghab. They're saying Sotis conspired to ship the material even though he knew he didn't have a permit, that Libya was on the "no go" list for restricted technology and that rebreathers were on that restricted list: "The purpose and object of the conspiracy was for the defendants to unlawfully transfer goods to be exported from the United States to Libya without a license, and in doing so evade U.S. export controls." This is not a minor charge. This is the most serious charge Sotis may have ever faced. The prosecutor is asking for 35 years' imprisonment, 11 years of supervised release and a $1.5 million fine.

Of course Peter Sotis denies the charges and says he will fight this to the end. He's confident he can beat the charges. If he doesn't, he may very well spend the rest of his days in jail.

EPILOGUE

Almost a year after Rob Stewart drowned, when I started filming my documentary, one of the first events I decided to shoot was one called *Saving our Seas from a Mile High*, put on by a shark conservation group in Denver called Fins Attached: Marine Research and Conservation. I wanted to film this because Sea Shepherd founder Paul Watson was going to be the keynote speaker and I was anxious to interview him both about his experiences as an environmentalist and his relationship with Rob Stewart. But I also wanted to meet some of the key people in Stewart's life – his parents would be attending, his friend Brock Cahill and possibly some of the members of his inner circle. It would be a chance to meet and greet and perhaps build some bridges that might help me down the line. I'd met with the Stewarts on two previous occasions to talk and ask about an interview, and while they hadn't said no, they also hadn't agreed to anything yet. So I was keen to keep working on that relationship. But Denver turned out to have significance beyond what I'd anticipated. It showed me first hand just how passionate people were about Rob Stewart. The evening event at a downtown Denver hotel had attracted several hundred people. Booths were set up in the hallway selling everything from shark T-shirts to key chains to memberships in various environmental organizations. It was everything you could imagine about saving sharks specifically and the oceans in general. The large main ballroom of the hotel had been set up to host Watson's speech and offer a silent auction that would raise money for the environmental group hosting the conference. It was an impressive event, and though we were initially viewed somewhat suspiciously by many of the attendees, they soon warmed up to us. In fact many people took time to talk with us to make sure we understood just how important Rob Stewart's work had been, and though they were passionate about saving everything to do with the oceans, like Rob Stewart, many had a particular place for sharks in their hearts and souls. One person came dressed in a shark costume. Watson spoke and the crowd cheered. Stewart's parents and friends spoke and they cheered even louder.

By the end of the evening, I was left with one overwhelming impression: Rob Stewart wasn't just a filmmaker or an environmentalist, he was a sort of beloved high priest of a group of environmental zealots. They loved him. They loved what he had done and they believed his accomplishments would never be forgotten. In a way I was really glad that I started my documentary with that shoot. It left a lasting impression on me about how important this man was to so many people. It was a fact that I would always keep in mind throughout my filming, regardless of what else I discovered about the circumstances surrounding his death. No one could take away what Stewart had accomplished and the lasting legacy that he left with these people. Stewart's parents showed a clip that night of the latest film Rob Stewart had been working on. They assured the crowd that they would not let his work just drop by the wayside, that they had assembled a team that would complete the film: Brian Stewart said, "We're absolutely committed. It's about half shot right now and the crew was in Bimini last week, shooting some young kids swimming with sharks, as one of the sequences in the movie.... Fortunately, we have all Rob's notes and he was very meticulous about planning every stage of the movie and writing out the story and describing what he was trying to achieve."

True to their promise, in the fall of 2018, *Sharkwater Extinction* was released in theatres in the United States and Canada. Reviews were mostly favourable. In fact its Metascore was slightly higher than the original documentary *Sharkwater*. But it didn't seem to garner the same kind of adoration that the original had. Possibly it was unrealistic that it ever could. In fact *Sharkwater Extinction* took some rather sharp criticism. Matt Zoller Seitz at RogerEbert.com observed:

> The film is so effective at generating outrage that one wishes it had taken a few steps back sometimes, to put more context around the offenses and crimes that it shows us. Although Stewart and his team do activist work in Los Angeles and off the coast of Florida, most of their efforts are focused on majority-nonwhite countries in Latin America, Asia, and Africa, where the fishing

population tends to be working class or poor. Absent any meaningful attempt to address the optics of the confrontations in this movie (and its predecessor) it often feels as if we're watching crusading white people trying to stop nonwhite people from eking out a precarious living, in a global economy ruled by stateless corporations that don't care about anything but bigger profits for the already-wealthy.

That observation resonated with me when I finally saw the movie. A little context about the Third World fishers and the fact that they're trapped between feeding their families and protecting fish species would have gone a long way. Nick Schager of *Variety* suggested, "There's a slight unseemliness to the film's treatment of Stewart's passing as something of a dramatic bombshell." But I understood Stewart's parents' desire to make the film somewhat of an homage to their son. Frank Scheck of the *Hollywood Reporter* wrote, "There's a scattershot quality to the proceedings, presumably caused by the Canadian writer-director not living long enough to complete the doc. But the individual segments register powerfully and the underwater sequences are beautifully shot, providing ample compensation for the narrative choppiness." The prestigious *New York Times* critic, Glenn Kenny, stated, "In his narration, Stewart recounts how he thought that if his films could make people love these animals, he could push popular opinion against their being hunted. He doesn't quite pull this off here, despite impressive footage of him swimming with sharks."

But others were far kinder. Janet Smith of the *Georgia Straight* said, "The most lasting imagery from *Sharkwater Extinction* are the more beautiful moments, shot in gorgeous high definition by 8K cameras. Free-diving with curious oceanic white tips and prehistoric-looking hammerhead in a shallow bay, Stewart comes across as some kind of shark whisperer – and takes us places most of us would never otherwise see." The review that most resonated with me was one written by John Bleasdale in *CineVue*: "According to Stewart, 99% of the shark population has been destroyed in the last three decades, with 100 million sharks killed each year. With such alarming figures cited, it'd be good to have the sources and authorities backing it up on-screen."

Overall, I loved the documentary. I thought it was arguably a better piece of craftsmanship than the original, but the journalist in me found it alarming that so many grand statements were made in the documentary without even a token effort at providing sources: 150 million sharks killed each year: I kept wanting to know, "according to whom?" Pictures of boats in Costa Rica described as "mafia" boats with no evidence offered about how Stewart knew this damning fact. A grand statement made that eliminating sharks will have a massive impact on our environment, but no suggestion of why or how that will happen. I would like to have known the connection between eliminating sharks and humanity's extinction, beyond vague ominous statements about the consequences of killing off apex predators. For me, a little evidence would have gone a long way and ultimately made the film stronger.

Regardless, the film, though not the viral hit of the original, picked up a half a dozen nominations and wins at various film festivals around the world – well short of the 13 wins and 3 nominations of the original according to the media website IMDb. What was particularly surprising, though, was that both Box Office Mojo and The Numbers suggested the film fared poorly at the box office. Both websites list the worldwide revenue of Sharkwater Extinction as a modest $1713.00 (still sitting at the same amount on March 13, 2020). That kind of money wouldn't pay the cost of a film crew for one day. If true, it suggested that a lot of money was spent and little made back. Compare that to what IMDb says about the original *Sharkwater* movie – it picked up $850,920 in U.S. release and $292,608 worldwide. That's amazing revenue for a documentary project. Of course *Sharkwater Extinction* will still make money from direct sales on iTunes and on the Sharkwater website, and there may be resales to international broadcasters that will bring in money.

But Rob Stewart's legacy won't rest on his final work. It will certainly be made up of the three documentary projects he completed during his life and the impact that first iconic piece, *Sharkwater*, had on the world. It was monumental. Speaking in Florida, just after Stewart's death, his mother Sandy said, "He had a six-year plan for changing the world." His father Brian added, "He had a belief that if he could teach people about nature and living in harmony with nature, the world would be a so much better place, and that was his objective, creating a balance between what man's needs are and what nature's needs are and to disregard all of nature's needs consistently is going to be the ultimate demise of mankind." During our conversation in Denver, noted environmentalist Paul Watson remembered Stewart fondly and declared he was a genuine eco-warrior, and he added that Stewart was an epic figure in the environmental movement. "I would say that he certainly has helped saved sharks. You know, I wouldn't look at it as a, on a species basis but certainly overall, it's an enormous educational achievement. I guess it would be sort of equivalent to what Jacques Cousteau was able to do back in the '60s, to elevate that public awareness." I challenged Watson on that comparison with Cousteau. "A little over the top?" I queried. But he adamantly defended that position and ultimately I think he's right. The two men accomplished very different things with their lives, but both broke through to the general public about the natural world in way that is almost unique. I can only think of one other person who has grabbed popular attention about nature in the way that Stewart and Cousteau accomplished: Sir David Attenborough with his series on the planet. Stewart's friend and fellow shark enthusiast, Chris Harvey-Clark, took a more down-home attitude when it came to remembering Rob Stewart:

> I mean eco-warrior, hero, all these terms get thrown around so much they've ceased to have a lot of impact on me. I really look at what somebody really did, what did they really do, and to me ... Rob's *Sharkwater* changed the way a generation felt about sharks and about marine [life], and then about marine conservation.... He took people like that and made them care about things that they never cared about before. To me, that's way better than eco-warrior. That is, you've changed, you've changed the perspective of a generation and ... to me, it's much more powerful. I mean warriors go to battle and die but people who are able to make a change like that, far superior to laying down your life, for whatever reason, is to make a lasting change that's beneficial to man.

Yet Harvey-Clark ultimately believed that what happened to Rob Stewart was almost inevitable. In fact there are hints in *Sharkwater Extinction* that suggested Stewart felt the same way. He had lived such an extreme life in his pursuit of wonderful images of his beloved sharks. He had taken risks in his attempts to get hard proof about the gangsters who were slaughtering them off. No risk was too severe, no chance too risky, to save a species, to save the oceans. Stewart spoke about the number of times he had come close to death, and each time he cheated it, he suggested in the documentary, he had more confidence that he would continue to survive these harrowing incidents. Harvey-Clark thinks that's the way it has to be in the pursuit of the exceptional. "I don't think there's any doubt that if you're going to max out, if you're going to put out everything you've got, then you're out on the edge, right, you're not, you're not running with the pack anymore, you're going to achieve greater things but you're also going to incur greater risks, and I think that's what happened with Rob, yeah, he wasn't running with the pack."

When I first started working on this investigation I spent a lot of time absorbing what Rob Stewart had produced – his documentaries, his book. I talked with as many of his friends as I could. The overriding image that kept popping into my mind was the image of Icarus. He was the son of Daedalus, the great ancient Greek engineer. Daedalus had been brought to the island of Crete to build a great maze where the Minotaur would live. But, not wanting the world to ever find out the secrets of the maze, the King of Crete kept Daedalus and his son Icarus trapped on the island. So Daedalus built a set of wings for each of them made of wax. He warned his son not to fly too close to the sea or the sun – the wings might melt. But once Icarus took to the air, driven by the exhilaration of flying and the pure curiosity to see how high he could go, he flew too close to the sun, his wings melted and he fell to his death. I felt that Rob Stewart was a little like Icarus – driven by his love of sharks and the ocean, his love of filmmaking, he pushed himself further and further, deeper and deeper, to find the best images, the most exceptional experiences for his audience. Ultimately that cost him his life. Harvey-Clark likes the metaphor, but amends it slightly. "It's funny, the Icarus image.... He was a creature of the sea, Rob.... His wax wings weren't melting as he flew closer to the sun ... but he was out on the edge and he was getting close to things most people never dream of or see, and very sadly, he paid the price for that, or an unfair price. Many people fly to that limit and come back and it was Rob's unfortunate luck not to."

LIST OF SOURCES

INTERVIEWS

Dr. Tom Beaver

Rob Bleser

Jack Bridges, KLVFD

Jonah Bryson

Michael Buckley

Brock Cahill

David Concannon

David Goodhue

Dr. Dean Grubbs

Chris Harvey-Clark

Lamar Hires, Dive Rite

Captain Jeff Janszen, United States Coast Guard

Lieutenant Commander Ryan Kelley, United States Coast Guard

Linda Kruszka

Steve Lewis

Lani Lum

Greg McFall, NOAA

Neal Pollock

Commander Clinton Prindle, United States Coast Guard

Dr. Claudia Sotis

Peter Sotis

Paul Watson

EMAILS

Between Jack Bridges, KLVFD and Michael Pizzio, March 7, 2017 (Bleser's status with the department).

Between Agent Brent Wagner and Emile Voissen, August 25, 2016.

Between Brock Cahill and author, October 15, 2019.

Brock Cahill, December 5, 2016, cited in rEvo Motion to Dismiss.

Dr. Thomas Beaver to Chief Don Bock, February 1, 2017 and February 21, 2017.

Karen Shaw, December 15, 2016, cited in rEvo Motion to Dismiss.

COURT DOCUMENTS

Horizon Dive Adventures, Inc. v. Sotis and Stewart, US District Court, Southern District of Florida, Case No. 4:17-Cv-10050-Jlk (Federal Case).

- Horizon Dive Adventures, Inc.'s Privilege Log Additional
- rEvo BVBA's Memorandum of Law in Support of Its Motion to Intervene, July 24, 2018.
- Brock Cahill deposition
- Dan Dawson deposition
- Jeff Knapp deposition
- Bobby Steele deposition
- David Wilkerson deposition

Sotis v Robotka, Broward County Civil Court, Case No. CACE-16-023011.

- Complaint (includes statements about Chinese tanks and Libyan sales)

Stewart v. Sotis et al., Broward County Civil Court, Case No. CACE-17-005915

- rEvo BVBA's Motion to Dismiss, 2019
- Second Amended Complaint, January 28, 2019
- Third Amended Complaint, January 6, 2020

USA v. Sotis, US District Court, Southern District of Florida, Case No. 19-20693, October 24, 2019.

REPORTS AND PUBLIC DOCUMENTS

Dan Warkander, "The CO_2 Scrubber in a Diver's Rebreather," Shearwater Research Paper, June 26, 2017.

Dr. Thomas Beaver, Medical Examiner's Report, Report of Post Mortem Examination, 17-0031.

Dr. Thomas Beaver, Death Record Medical Information Sheet (Noah Cullen), August 7, 2015.

Monroe County Sheriff Report, MCS0140FF006047, 08/04/2014 to 08/07/2015. Noah Cullen.

Monroe County Police Report, MSC0170FF000760. Rob Stewart.

Navy Experimental Diving Unit (NEDU) report, 3963/17-15, Ser 03/018, April 17, 2017.

Sworn Affidavit of Sergeant Mark Coleman dated October 18, 2018.

PUBLISHED MATERIAL

Bleasdale, John. https://cine-vue.com/2019/03/film-review-sharkwater -extinction.html.

Kenny, Glenn. https://www.nytimes.com/2019/02/28/movies/sharkwater -extinction-review.html.

NOAA Diving Manual, 6th ed. North Palm Beach, FL: Best Publishing, 2017.

Scheck, Frank. https://www.hollywoodreporter.com/review/sharkwater -extinction-1191462.

Smith, Janet. https://www.straight.com/movies/1151426/sharkwater -extinction-gives-rob-stewart-epitaph-he-deserves.

Stewart, Rob. *Save the Humans*. Toronto: Random House Canada, 2012.

Zoller Seitz, Matt. https://www.rogerebert.com/reviews/sharkwater -extinction-2019.